Myrtle Beach

Myrtle Beach

by
Liz and Charlie Mitchell

Myrtle Beach, 2nd Edition (*Tourist Town Guides*®)
© 2010 by Liz and Charlie Mitchell

Published by:
Channel Lake, Inc., P.O. Box 1771, New York, NY 10156-1771
http://www.channellake.com

Authors: Liz and Charlie Mitchell
Editorial & Layout: Quadrum Solutions (http://www.quadrumltd.com)
Cover Design: Julianna Lee
Front Cover Photos:
"Good Golf Day" © iStockphoto.com/andykazie
"The Beach" © Liz and Charlie Mitchell
"Golf clubs in bag" © iStockphoto.com/TRITOOTH
Back Cover Photos:
"Brookgreen Gardens" © Liz and Charlie Mitchell

Published in April, 2010

ISBN-13: 978-1-935455-01-1

Disclaimer: The information in this book has been checked for accuracy. However, neither the publisher nor the author may be held liable for errors or omissions. *Use this book at your own risk.* To obtain the latest information, we recommend that you contact the vendors directly. If you do find an error, let us know at corrections@channellake.com

Channel Lake, Inc. is not affiliated with the vendors mentioned in this book, and the vendors have not authorized, approved or endorsed the information contained herein. This book contains the opinions of the author, and your experience may vary.

For more information, visit http://www.touristtown.com

Help Our Environment!

Even when on vacation, your responsibility to protect the environment does not end. Here are some ways you can help our planet without spoiling your fun:

★ Ask your hotel staff not to clean your towels and bed linens each day. This reduces water waste and detergent pollution.

★ Turn off the lights, heater, and/or air conditioner when you leave your hotel room, and keep that thermostat low!

★ Use public transportation when available. Tourist trolleys are very popular, and they are usually cheaper and easier than a car.

★ Recycle everything you can, and properly dispose of rubbish in labeled receptacles.

Tourist towns consume a lot of energy. Have fun, but don't be wasteful. Please do your part to ensure that these attractions are around for future generations to visit and enjoy.

Before it was officially called Myrtle Beach, the region went by the name of New Town.

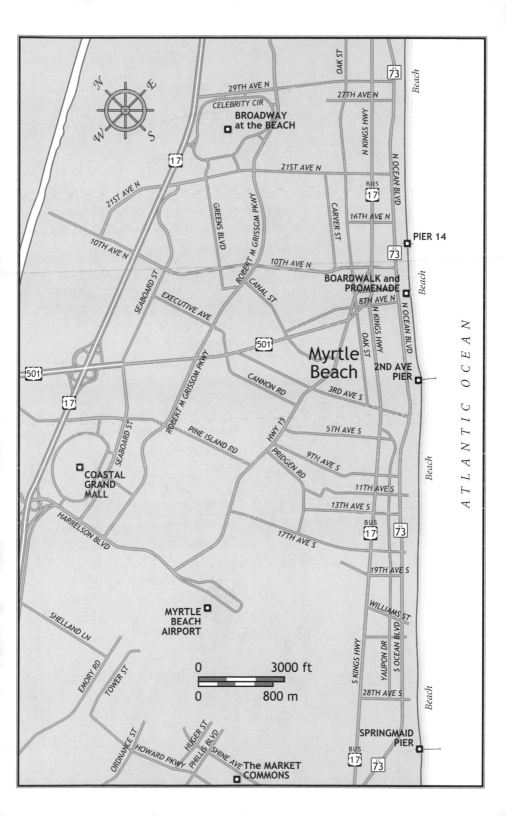

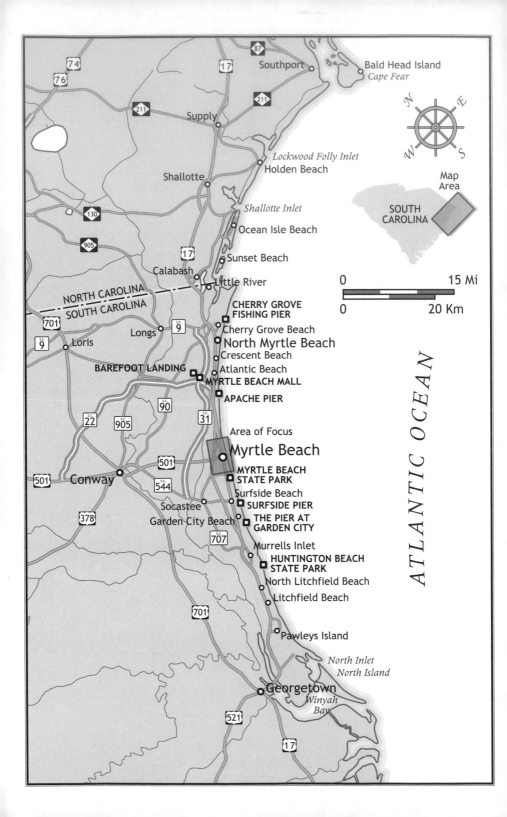

Table of Contents

How to Use this Book

Tourist Town Guides® makes it easy to find exactly what you are looking for! Just flip to a chapter or section that interests you. The tabs on the margins will help you find your way quickly.

Attractions are usually listed by subject groups. Attractions may have an address, Web site (🖱), and/or telephone number (☎) listed.

Must-See Attractions: Headlining must-see attractions, or those that are otherwise iconic or defining, are designated with the ✪ **Must See!** symbol.

Coverage: This book is not all-inclusive. It is comprehensive, with many different options for entertainment, dining, shopping, etc. but there are many establishments not listed here.

Prices: At the end of many attraction listings is a general pricing reference, indicated by dollar signs, relative to other attractions in the region. The scale is from "$" (least expensive) to "$$$" (most expensive). Contact the attraction directly for specific pricing information.

*Myrtle Beach got its name in 1938
courtesy of a contest, when Franklin
Burroughs' wife suggested the name to
represent the prolific wax myrtle trees
that grow in abundance here.*

Welcome to Myrtle Beach

Welcome to the Myrtle Beach area of South Carolina. One of America's top beach destinations with attractions, entertainment, shopping, lodging, and dining to please any visitor, Myrtle Beach is a year-round tourist destination. Guests head to Myrtle Beach for fun and relaxation. It's big and bold, and flashes more neon than a handful of other popular beaches combined. It might slow down, but it never stops.

Myrtle Beach is one of America's favorite vacation destinations. It's part of the Grand Strand which is a 60-mile strip of South Carolina beach along the Atlantic Ocean, free for public use and always open. The beautiful beach is clean, wide, and safe for sun, sport, and water lovers. Temperate climate and sunny days encourage outdoor play.

The area is a popular spot for families who enjoy a wide variety of attractions ranging from miniature golf to amusement parks and educational programs. High quality entertainment is available for music lovers of any age or interest.

Festivals deliver opportunities for locals and guests to mingle in frequent celebrations of cuisine and culture. Delectable dishes in hundreds of eateries feature fresh seafood and regional specialties for fine dining or casual meals.

Golfers play year-round with more than 70 championship courses designed by some of the world's most notable names. Anglers choose inshore or Gulf Stream fishing for dozens of species.

Myrtle Beach is big and bold with tourism as its main business, and visitors can expect a genuine warm welcome from friendly southerners. Everyone can find something to love with a Myrtle Beach visit.

PLANNING THE TRIP

Reservations for lodging should be made before arriving in Myrtle Beach. Although there are more than 90,000 rooms available across hotels, condos, villas, rental houses, and campgrounds in the Grand Stand area, it may be difficult to find accommodation during the summer season, particularly between Memorial Day and Labor Day without advance planning. For last-minute visits during the busiest season, it is more likely that accommodations will be available at the north or south ends of the Grand Strand rather than in the heart of either Myrtle Beach or North Myrtle Beach.

Telephone or online reservations are advised. Many of the recommended accommodations are locally owned rather than chains. With large chain hotels, the toll free number will be available on the web site, but it is possible that the line will be answered in a central location for that particular chain rather than in the actual property in the Myrtle Beach area. Keeping that in mind, the toll free numbers may be convenient strictly for reservations, but not for any information about local events in the area nearby. For any special needs or individual questions, a phone call to the local property is suggested.

Dining reservations before arriving in the area are not necessary, but are suggested on arrival if specific restaurants are chosen for fine dining or for groups larger than eight.

Pack shorts, tee shirts, bathing suits and cover-ups for a visit to the beach any time of year. Winter months are not always warm enough for wearing shorts or short sleeves every day, but it is good to be prepared for warm weather anytime of the year; it wouldn't be a huge surprise to be able to walk along the beach on New Year's Eve in shorts. The ocean temperature is not comfortable for swimming during the few months of winter, but many accommodations have indoor pools or hot tubs. A jacket or sweatshirt is often handy for evening walks on the beach, but not needed during the summer unless restaurant air conditioning is too cold.

A hat or cap and sunscreen are important for long visits to the beach and are easily available locally as well.

Flip flops or sandals are important for protecting the feet during a beach visit. Buy them at any beachwear, grocery or other retail store on arrival if they don't arrive in the suitcase. They form a significant part of a beach wardrobe at Myrtle Beach because the pavement can sometimes get steaming hot and there is a chance of getting the feet hurt on the sea shells that wash up on the beach. Sand spurs are a type of tiny prickly weed sprinkled in the sand along some of the coast, and they really hurt if accidentally attached to feet. Flip flops, sandals or shoes should be worn for safety and foot care. Avoid wearing socks with sandals, especially gentlemen in shorts wearing dark socks with sandals. It is the surest sign of a tourist, because locals generally go sockless almost year-round.

Dining is casual in most places, and tourists are inclined to wear shorts and tee shirts everywhere. Dressy casuals such as khaki slacks with a sport jacket for gentlemen, and a pair of slacks or dresses for ladies may be comfortable attire for theater visits or a few of the upscale restaurants, although it is not required.

For those tourists interested in playing a few rounds of golf, collared shirts and golf shorts are acceptable for both men and women, while tee shirts, short shorts and jeans might not be suitable. See the "Golf" chapter for any recommendations of attire for specific local courses.

Pack a camera or pick up a disposable one at any retail store. Golden sunsets, picturesque scenery and unforgettable memories will be worth capturing on a Myrtle Beach visit.

GETTING TO MYRTLE BEACH

Getting to Myrtle Beach is easy by air or road. Most visitors drive because it helps to have a car on arrival. Although this area is not directly on an Interstate highway, I-95, which runs north-south throughout the United States, is less than an hour from Myrtle Beach. New highways were built around Myrtle Beach during the early 2000s, so that visitors would have good choices for driving in from the west and for moving directly between north and south.

ARRIVING BY CAR

I-40, which runs east-west across the United States, also offers an easy connection to U.S. 17 leading directly south to Myrtle Beach. Although a slow route traveling through many small towns, U.S. 17 offers direct access into Myrtle Beach from Georgia and Florida to the south and from North Carolina, Virginia and other states to the northeast. U.S. 22, called Veteran's Highway, arrives directly into Myrtle Beach from the west. U.S. 31 runs north-south from Little River to Socastee and crosses U.S. 22 for access to Myrtle Beach, North Myrtle Beach, and Surfside.

ARRIVING BY AIR

The Myrtle Beach International Airport (MYR) is in the city itself. Major airlines are Delta connections ASA and ComAir, Continental, Allegiant, United, Northwest, Spirit Air, and US Air with daily flights that vary seasonally. Connections via Atlanta, New York, and Charlotte provide convenient international links. Additional regional airlines such as Myrtle Beach Direct Air also offer service. Porter Air direct flights from Toronto were announced in late 2009 and are set to begin daily service in spring 2010.

If arriving by air into Myrtle Beach, booking a rental car in advance is recommended, as public transportation within the area is limited, and having a car helps unless the visit is contained entirely within one property. Car rentals on the airport property are Avis, Thrifty, Sears, Budget, Alamo, Hertz, and Ace. A limited number of taxis are usually on-site for pick-ups at the airport.

Shuttles from many major accommodations may be arranged for airport transfers. Confirming the pick-up schedule with the accommodation before arrival is advisable.

GETTING AROUND

It's easy to get around by car in the Myrtle Beach area, as long as the heavy traffic anticipated on the main routes during the busy summer tourist season do not act as a deterrent. While the city of Myrtle Beach is actually quite small, the entire Grand Strand area includes a 60-mile strip of coast, all of which is considered to be a vacation spot and has been described in this book.

Due to the extensive length of the Grand Strand, it's most convenient to choose daily dining and the majority of golf within the geographic section near the lodging.

While traveling in the area, one important thing to remember is that Myrtle Beach and North Myrtle Beach are two separate neighboring cities, though some of the east-west streets have the same names or numbers. This can be quite confusing if a new visitor does not know which city is being referenced. In both cities, the cross streets (east-west) are numbered beginning in the center of the city and extending both northward and southward. For instance, 10th could refer to 10th Ave. N. or 10th Ave. S. in Myrtle Beach, or to 10th Ave. N. or 10th Ave. S. in North Myrtle Beach! Similar street numbering is also used in Garden City, Conway, and the other small towns in the area. Confusing? It is, when it comes without a reference to the locality; then it becomes apparent that it's logical and easy to follow.

U.S. 17, which runs north-south through the entire Grand Strand, is locally dubbed the Bypass for five miles around Myrtle Beach. This is one of the most confusing locations for a first-time visitor, as there is no sign that actually denotes Bypass, although verbal directions and sometimes published business addresses use the term. The so-called Bypass is an alternate route to U.S. Business 17 which runs parallel to it, and they join both at the northern and southern ends.

WHO VISITS MYRTLE BEACH

The Myrtle Beach area attracts an estimated 15 million visitors each year. As many as three million of these are international guests, primarily from countries such as Canada, England, and Germany. The majority travel from North Carolina, Ohio, and the Midwest, northeast, and Mid-Atlantic States.

Summer is the peak season for families, beginning with the Memorial Day weekend in late May, and ending with Labor Day, the first weekend of September. During the summer season, lodging rates are the highest, major restaurants are extremely busy, and all attractions are fully operational for long hours. Malls, shopping outlets, and major retailers stay open through the evening, sometimes as late as 11:00 p.m. In addition to the beach and free activities, plenty of other affordable attractions and amusements are suitable for children such as miniature golf. See the "Attractions" chapter for additional suggestions.

Young couples without children or families who especially crave the hot summer weather also choose this season for the best beach escapes. It is the ideal time to get away from colder climates.

High school graduates from neighboring states such as North Carolina and Virginia, as well as throughout South Carolina, often celebrate their new-found freedom with Senior Week at Myrtle Beach. The tradition is unofficial, yet expected and welcomed by many of the beach establishments. Specific events are not offered, and each group of graduating seniors plans their own trip which many view as a rite of passage. Law enforcement authorities are particularly watchful to discourage underage drinking and reckless behavior. Many hotels and rental agencies will not rent to teenagers without the authority of an adult. College students, especially from South Carolina, often spend summers at the beach where temporary jobs are available.

Golfers visit during the spring and fall, with the peak golfing seasons being determined by the perfect weather and ideal condition of the courses. April and October offer excellent golfing. With no danger of morning frost, daylight hours are long enough for the serious player or amateur to enjoy 36 holes in a day. Visiting golfers come to Myrtle Beach from all over the world. Golf rates are high, but lodging rates are lower than during the summer. Packages that include accommodation and golf choices are a suitable deal for almost any budget.

Baby boomers also visit during spring and fall, with or without the attraction of golfing. Without the demand for all water sports or long days on the beach, temperatures are ideal for some sunning, swimming, walking and all of the other activities. The days are gorgeous, the sunsets are special, and there are no long queues waiting to get into restaurants or clubs.

One specific segment of boomers includes the dancers, known as shaggers, who come for the events during spring and fall which are filled with beach music, contests, parades, and plenty of dancing and partying day and night.

Traditional American holidays, such as Thanksgiving, Christmas, and Easter, find a few families traveling to Myrtle Beach for reunions. These are seen as easy times to avoid the crowds and take advantage of the amenities. Fresh seafood prepared by a Myrtle Beach chef can be arranged as well for those who want a taste of the local cuisine. With the exception of the traditional Friday after a nationwide Thanksgiving shopping frenzy, other days are devoid of heavy crowds for fall and winter browsing through the outlet centers, malls, and boutiques. Visitors from other sections of South Carolina and rural North Carolina areas frequent the Myrtle Beach shopping districts for buys which are not to be found elsewhere.

Winter is the slowest time of year in the Myrtle Beach area. It's also the favored time for retirees. The group, dubbed snow birds, generally lives here for two or three months at a stretch, beginning right after Christmas, or take their extended vacations during January or February. Accommodation rates are at their absolute lowest, and a week may be as inexpensive as a night during the high season. It's not hot beach weather, but the temperatures rarely compare to northeast or Canadian winters.

Groups who travel with planned motorcoach tours also frequent all coastal destinations during the winter. February is the best month for entertainment in the Myrtle Beach theaters. After seasonal performances end, theaters typically remain closed during January. Therefore, the talent is fresh and new acts are presented when the theaters reopen for the annual season in February. Accommodation rates are also geared for discounts courting group visits during this period.

Meetings and conventions also bring popular visitors to Myrtle Beach during winter. Rates are attractive, crowds are not a concern, and businesses welcome the attention. Anyone who lives away from the coast finds the views equally attractive, with walks on the beach and fresh seafood in the restaurants surpassing many competing business destinations.

Turtle watches are another significant source of attraction along many of the less inhabited sections of the coast. The residents take the task of turtle watching very seriously due to the fear of extinction resulting from coastal erosion, construction, and commercial fishing as well as from predators. The loggerhead turtle comes ashore to deposit her eggs. The nests are sought for careful guarding by humans to prevent scavenging wildlife from destroying them. Upon the eggs hatching, volunteers shepherd the tiny creatures toward their home in the sea. With a little bit of help, they can grow to be 300-pound sea turtles. Bald Head Island is recognized nationally for its sea turtle nesting program, documenting more than 100 nests in a recent year. Evening turtle walks coordinated by volunteers on several of the small islands are sometimes the highlight for beach visitors.

Myrtle Beach is usually thought of as a middle-class destination, but it also offers some upscale penthouses or rental and second homes. Fine dining appeals to the wealthy who can arrive via their own jet or dock their yacht where permitted. Nationally known stars who frequently play at the local theaters never complain to their limousine driver that they want Myrtle Beach off their tour!

Who comes to Myrtle Beach? Everyone loves to visit here. For some it's a once in a lifetime trip to a notable coastal destination. For others, it's a tradition which is passed down through generations, gaining friends along the way.

Area Orientation

The Myrtle Beach area was first a Native American trail inhabited by the Winyah and Waccamaw who called it Chicora. It was sometime in the 1500s that Spanish explorers sailed from Hispaniola with Lucas Vacquez de Allyon. The first European settlement in the United States, San Miguel de Guadalupe, was 30 miles south of the present Myrtle Beach. It lasted less than a year with settlers dying from hardship and disease.

President George Washington's travels through the area were documented in his diary of April 1791, while he was touring the southern states.

As far as historical significance goes, the Myrtle Beach area can claim little and is fairly recently developed. It is further south in South Carolina in the cities of Charleston and Beaufort that history lovers can satiate their appetite for the past and find structures dating back a 100 years or more. A 65-acre historic district located along north Ocean Boulevard and listed on the National Register of Historic Places is distinguished by private homes built from the 1920s through the 1940s.

The Myrtle Beach area first came into prominence when wealthy families began sending their women and children to the coast to escape the inland heat and humidity of the summer season. Franklin Burroughs returned here from the Civil War and began a timber and turpentine company with his friend Benjamin Collins.

The construction of a railroad spurred activity among farmers and also led to the development of additional industries. The

Myrtle Beach Train Depot, also listed on the National Register, was built in 1936 and restored in 2004. It is now used as an event venue.

Myrtle Beach was so named in 1938 in a contest, when Burroughs' wife suggested the name to represent the prolific wax myrtle trees. It became a city nearly two decades after that in 1957.

NORTH MYRTLE BEACH

The railroad created the connection to what is now the city of North Myrtle Beach, which was created in 1968 by joining the beach communities of Windy Hill, Crescent Beach, Ocean Drive, and Cherry Grove. Although not actually marked as such on any signboard, locals often offer directions or discuss these areas.

Vanna White is North Myrtle Beach's celebrity connection. Recognized as a letter turner and hand clapper since 1982 on the long-running television show *Wheel of Fortune*, White was born in North Myrtle Beach in 1957. She occasionally returns to her beachfront home, and makes frequent appearances in local celebrity events.

THE GRAND STRAND

The term Grand Strand was coined for the first time in 1949 by Claude Dunnagan, as the title for a newspaper column. While Grand Strand is not actually on the map, it is used locally to refer to the 60-mile strip of beach, which runs from Georgetown to Little River at the North Carolina border.

ATLANTIC BEACH

Atlantic Beach is a tiny town, less than half a square mile in size with slightly more than 100 households. Dubbed "The Black Pearl," it was the only South Carolina beach which was open to African-Americans during the years of segregation. Families from across the state began traveling here during the 1930s and continued to do so for several decades, to enjoy the music and dancing and the warm welcome they always received. It was incorporated as a town in 1966.

The beach itself remains disconnected from the adjacent beaches to the north and south. Falling into disrepair, the town suffered from many years of neglect in spite of annual festivals attempting to generate funds, and occasional investors with ideas for ambitious projects in an effort to preserve the town's culture and traditions. Investors and residents are discussing ways to revive the town and restore its original glory.

HORRY COUNTY

Today the Myrtle Beach area denotes all of Horry County (pronounced O-Ree). The county was named for Peter Horry who was a Revolutionary War hero and wealthy plantation owner. Horry County is the largest county in South Carolina with 1,134 square miles.

Little River is across the Intracoastal Waterway from North Myrtle Beach. It's the northernmost coastal community of Horry County and is on the Atlantic Intracoastal Waterway, known as the river, rather than on the ocean. The north-south route between Wilmington and Myrtle Beach passes through the commercial strip of Little River, with a marina and a fishing village on the river, just a short drive off the main route.

Conway is the county seat and is located west of Myrtle Beach. It is on the way for many visitors driving from the north or west, although bypass roads have routed traffic around the small town. Quaint and historic, Conway hosts a walking tour that begins near the home of the town's visitor center. Seventeen structures in this town, which was established in 1732, are on the National Register of Historic Places. Some are from the early 1800s to the early 1900s, when most of the current town was built. The restored downtown area includes some shopping, with art and boutiques and dining in a few good restaurants. Details are in the "Events" chapter and the "Dining" chapter.

Loris and **Aynor** are small towns to the west of the North Myrtle Beach area. **Surfside Beach** is a town at the south of Myrtle Beach. **Garden City Beach** is a community at the far southern end of the Grand Strand, with the Georgetown County line beginning within Garden City.

CLIMATE AND TEMPERATURES

There is an average of 215 sunny days annually. The climate is subtropical, with year-round temperatures reported at an average of 63° Fahrenheit. It actually ranges from the 50s to the 60s in the winter and is in the mid- to high-80s during the summer. Spring and fall, such as April and October, usually average in the 80s. Coastal temperatures are several degrees cooler than the inland regions due to the ocean breeze. Average water temperature is 66° Fahrenheit.

BEYOND MYRTLE BEACH

While visiting Myrtle Beach and the surrounding towns and beaches that are part of the Grand Strand, travelers will find additional sights and attractions if they venture a bit farther to the west, north or south. For visitors who prefer to soak up some history or want to spend a few days out of the sun, a few special choices can be considered, any of which offer opportunities for a day trip or a stopover to or from vacation.

BRUNSWICK COUNTY

Brunswick County, North Carolina, is the neighbor to the immediate north of Myrtle Beach. Family beaches in Brunswick County attract many summer visitors who like less activity on their spot of sand, yet prefer to be close to the entertainment and amenities. These beaches are within an hour's drive to the major part of Myrtle Beach, but seem to be years removed from the crowds and the activity. Accommodation here includes rental houses, villas, and condos along with an occasional hotel or bed and breakfast. Several are actually small barrier islands situated between the Atlantic Ocean and the Intracoastal Waterway. All of these islands have fishing piers, marinas, fresh seafood stands, local eateries, and enough free beach space to accommodate walkers, swimmers, and sunbathers.

HOLDEN BEACH

Holden Beach is noted for fishing with its prime season usually marked by spring and fall festivals packed with craft and food vendors and entertainers. Proximity to golf courses and availability of water sports are added benefits for visitors.

OCEAN ISLE BEACH

Ocean Isle Beach is the home of the annual North Carolina Oyster Festival in the third week of October. A large event promising every possible celebration of the mighty mollusk, this festival also hosts oyster-shucking contests and offers fried or stewed meals. Entertainment, craft stalls, and plenty of festival food to please the palate round out a full day when the weather is usually at the peak of fall perfection.

SOUTHPORT

The historic town of Southport overlooks the banks of the Cape Fear River where it empties into the Atlantic Ocean. Frequent waterfront events, plenty of local entertainment and cozy bed-and-breakfast inns abound. History lovers can view 2,000-year-old artifacts in the North Carolina Maritime Museum.

BALD HEAD ISLAND

Bald Head Island is an upscale getaway for golfers and vacationers. It's accessible only by private boat or by 20-minute ferry ride from the new Deep Point Marina in Southport. No cars are allowed on the island, which includes 10,000 acres preserved in its natural wild beauty.

SUNSET BEACH

Sunset Beach includes a three-mile strip which is connected to the mainland by a new bridge that replaced the antiquated bridge perched on pontoons for years. The **Ingram Planetarium** on the mainland in Sunset Beach features the third SkiDome in the world. Summer programs educate and entertain in a sophisticated theater equipped with HD projection. The science hall and planetarium dome are part of the **Museum of Coastal Carolina** which is based in neighboring Ocean Isle.

BIRD ISLAND

Bird Island is an uninhabited island which can only be reached by a walk from Sunset Beach. The mile-and-a-half of beach leads to the South Carolina border. Its only structure is a mailbox where visitors leave journals or notes, sometimes describing their viewing of nearly 260 species of birds documented here.

WILMINGTON

The city of Wilmington, just north of Brunswick County, is a day trip away and offers eclectic browsing and shopping, along with interesting dining fronting its scenic riverwalk. Restored cotton mills and manufacturing plants reflect the years gone by. Home to important film production for many years, Wilmington's reputation incorporates its historic development and modern culture.

BATTLESHIP NORTH CAROLINA

Across the bridge, which leads south from Wilmington toward Myrtle Beach, the Battleship North Carolina is a history buff's delight. A national monument, it stays open every day of the year. This is an authentically restored combat ship which was part of every major naval offensive in the Pacific. Interpretive signage is posted along portions of nine decks open for self-guided touring. Special events include living history demonstrations, ghost walks, fireworks, and entertainment.

GEORGETOWN COUNTY

Moving to the far south end beyond the Myrtle Beach area, Georgetown County is a welcome spot for fishing and water sports along the waterfront of historic Georgetown. One of the popular annual events here is the Wooden Boat Show on the third weekend in October. The 20-year-old event features a boat building challenge, maritime arts, crafts, and exhibits. Local entertainers, artists, and plenty of fresh seafood complete the festive day. Details are in the "Events" chapter.

CHARLESTON

Charleston is approximately two hours south of Myrtle Beach. For a day trip to one of the country's most important and best loved historic cities, this would be at the top of the list. Before reaching the city, vacationers can stop at **Boone Hall Plantation**, a working plantation open to visitors interested in learning about farm life over the past 300 years. Frequent events and entertainment also are hosted here.

Dining in Charleston is also an experience in itself, with renowned chefs serving the lowcountry's best seafood and fresh produce in their own concoctions.

DRAYTON HALL

Located within the city, Drayton Hall is America's oldest preserved plantation house, and is open for tours. The city is known for its wealthy settlers and its key role in the African-American experience in this country.

America's first museum showcases the natural and cultural history of the region. Churches and architecture are among the reasons to visit Charleston. Horse-drawn carriage tours provide narrated looks at the mansions and family stories hidden behind centuries-old iron gates. A variety of tours including plantation tours, nature tours, and ethnic tours offer a complete look at various facets of the region where the beautiful lowcountry of South Carolina begins. Moss-draped live oaks, magnolia blooms, and southern sweet tea are highlights of a visit here. In this city, sophisticated shopping sits comfortably alongside restored buildings in the historic downtown walking district, which is home to the campus of the College of Charleston.

June through December is hurricane season in Myrtle Beach, with September being the most common month of concern.

The Beach

The primary lure for visitors to the Myrtle Beach area is the beach itself. It's always open and enjoyable throughout the year. Though the water temperature is not comfortable for swimming during winter, other water sports, beach walks, shell-collecting, and bird-watching are activities that can be enjoyed any time of the year.

Easily accessible in many areas along the 60-mile strip known as the Grand Strand, the beach is wide, clean, and safe. The beach itself in the state of South Carolina is public property. However, gated or resort communities sometimes have private access to the beach fronting their property.

Myrtle Beach has nine and a half miles of beach, while the North Myrtle Beach is just a little shorter at nine miles. There is additional beach area in the towns of Surfside, Atlantic Beach, and an unincorporated area of the county between the cities.

In Myrtle Beach, the beachfront is easily accessible from dozens of hotels. The main section of town also has signposts at regular intervals indicating public access spots, many of which include free parking, albeit limited. Pay parking meters and private pay lots are located throughout several blocks in the main section. Parking meters are occasionally removed as a special treat for visitors during specific periods of the year, if you're fortunate to visit at the time.

Parking is free throughout South Carolina for properly tagged vehicles for handicapped, Purple Heart or disabled American veteran.

Like Myrtle Beach, North Myrtle Beach also has similar signs that denote public access points, and offer free public parking in a number of locations and free street parking in other spots. Oceanfront hotels with their own parking decks or lots offer immediate access to the beach.

Lifeguards and equipment rental during the primary summer season are managed by the cities of Myrtle Beach and North Myrtle Beach. Staff is on duty only during prime daytime hours. Some resort hotels on the beach employ private lifeguards and usually provide or rent beach chairs and umbrellas. Some beaches do not have lifeguards. Beach laws apply, irrespective of the staff being on or off duty.

QUICK TIPS

Remember to treat the beach with respect. Whether it's a public access beach or accessed via a privately owned resort property, it may have different rules or restrictions, but a few tips should be remembered as common courtesies.

DUNES

Nature's way of protecting the shore is washing sand up to create dunes. These get invariably damaged by walkers, sunbathers, or pets. In many locations, law prohibits walking on the dunes.

SEA OATS

Sometimes planted, at other times growing naturally, this lovely grass holds the sand in place along the dunes, and should not be disturbed.

PERSONAL SPACE

A typically American way of living is to allow personal space. Park your chair, umbrella, kids, and beach paraphernalia a reasonable distance away from others. Try to keep your music or phone calls not too loud and give the others privacy for conversation.

DOGS

Though allowed on some beaches, often with leashes, dogs may sometimes annoy non-owners. Their waste should be collected and disposed properly. Otherwise, it can be a health hazard.

DIGGING HOLES

Digging in the beach sand seems to be a natural pastime for kids and dogs, but holes should be filled when they have served their entertainment purpose. Otherwise, runners or other beach goers could miss seeing a deep hole, leading them to trip and fall.

TRASH ON THE BEACH

Leave the beach cleaner than you find it, and dispose the trash. In addition to creating a negative impression by leaving trash behind, trash is also a major danger to sea life.

PRIVATE PROPERTY

Straying onto the posted property of a neighboring resort or private owner may be illegal as well as considered a breach of etiquette.

SHELLS

Tiny, living creatures may still be hidden in shells which are found on the edge of the surf. Don't collect shells which are not dry and free of their inhabitants. If shells having live creatures are picked up, their inhabitants may crawl out to offer a surprise in a beach bag at home, or they will die and create an unpleasant odor.

FIREWORKS

Many public beach access areas post signage informing the public if fireworks are unlawful. Any questions about the differing laws throughout the various beaches should be directed to police officials, if not addressed on the web site of each individual city.

SEA GULLS

Don't feed the sea gulls. Research has shown that their feathers and droppings may have disease-carrying bacteria. If the birds are fed, they will fly closer to people and will not discriminate where their droppings may land.

ALLIGATORS

These amphibians are dangerous and should not be fed or approached. Other wildlife, such as deer, raccoons, or even black bears, is sometimes found in residential areas and should be avoided. Wildlife is known to carry disease-carrying bacteria, including the possibility of rabies.

LOGGERHEAD TURTLES

In danger of extinction, these creatures nest on the edge of the sand dunes and deposit eggs. The eggs hatch after 60 days, wherein tiny hatchlings emerge and try to find their way into the sea. State law prohibits disturbing the dunes, and the protection of wildlife is one of the important reasons for staying away from the restricted areas.

SUNSCREEN
Be sure to apply it frequently during beach visits, even on overcast days.

BABIES
Be careful about exposing little children, babies in particular, to extreme sun or heat.

DISABLED ACCESS
A limited number of beachgoing wheelchairs are free, and handicap access to beaches can be located in several sections in the central areas of Myrtle Beach. Information is available at ● *cityofmyrtlebeach.com*

ACTIVITIES AND RECREATION
Both the City of Myrtle Beach and North Myrtle Beach offer recreation classes and sports programs. Gyms offer opportunities to visitors to enjoy daily or short-term activities. See ● *cityofmyrtlebeach.com* and ● *n-myrtle-beach.sc.us* for details.

SURFING
Surf advisories are important, and swimmers should adhere to any weather warnings.

WEATHER SYSTEMS
The Atlantic can create dangerous rip currents. These are beneath the water surface and cannot be recognized until the

swimmer is caught in the strong current. Swimmers should check with local news media or lifeguards to stay abreast of any such issues. Any advisories of distance from shore or from lifeguard stand should be taken seriously.

HURRICANE SEASON

The period from June to December is the hurricane season, with September being the month most commonly of concern. Local emergency management offices are extremely sophisticated. In case of a serious hurricane threat, evacuation of part or all of the area may be recommended as voluntary or mandatory. Visitors should follow all such advice. During weather emergencies, water and electricity could be unavailable and streets blocked. Visitors or residents who disobey requests and advice to leave may inadvertently endanger the lives of others who might be called upon for rescue.

EMERGENCY

Service for fire, police and rescue is available via 911 throughout all parts of the Myrtle Beach area.

Summer at the Beach

Beach Chairs

Cherry Grove Pier

Golfing at Myrtle Beach

Home of the Shag

Shore Bird

Brookgreen Gardens

Marina

Murrells Inlet

Downtown Myrtle Beach

South Carolina's state dance, the Shag,
originated in North Myrtle Beach.

Attractions

Places to go and things to do are easy to find, whether for families with children, retirees, or any age between. The toughest part is deciding what to do on each visit. Many attractions and activities are open year-round, although outdoor venues are most enjoyable during clear weather with spring or fall temperatures. Rates and hours vary seasonally and from year to year. Most attractions offer senior citizens' and children's discounts. Some even offer military discounts. Price notes show comparisons among the attractions, ranging from free to an admission cost of least expensive ($), average ($$) or most expensive ($$$).

ALLIGATOR ADVENTURE
(Barefoot Landing, U.S. 17 ☎ 843.361.0789
▌ alligatoradventure.com) Called the reptile capital of the world, this attraction showcases many more species than the numerous alligators. Lectures detailing the history of these reptiles are conducted near a pool holding some 300 alligators. Tiny infant reptiles can sometimes be petted by visitors. From mid-April until mid-October, daily hand-feeding is one of the highlights for visitors. There are no shows during cooler months, because alligators don't eat then. The creatures live in swamps and marshes similar to their natural habitat. Apart from the abundance of alligators, tigers, lemurs, zebras, river otters, beavers, and tropical birds live here, in addition to snakes, Galapagos tortoises, turtles, and frogs. The largest crocodile in the United States also makes its home here. For those not satisfied with one visit, a second-day pass is available and offers a second visit within seven days. *($$)*

...ALK AND PROMENADE ⊘ Must See!

(Oceanfront ☎ 843.918.1000 ⛟ cityofmyrtlebeach.com) This new attraction set for completion in 2010 is a 1.2-mile stretch along the central section of beach, between the Second Avenue Pier and the 14th Avenue N. Pier. Way back in the 1910s and 1920s, an original ten-foot wide wooden boardwalk followed the dune line along the oceanfront for several blocks in both directions from the center of town. A combination of a park, beach, and shopping center, the promenade will showcase the beach views at the center of the city. *(Free)*

BROOKGREEN GARDENS ⊘ Must See!

(1931 Brookgreen Dr., Murrells Inlet ☎ 843.235.6000 ⛟ brookgreen.org) Apart from being an outdoor and indoor art exhibit, the garden museum also preserves and showcases natural flora and fauna. It was founded in 1931 by Archer and Anna Hyatt Huntington, and many among the hundreds of large sculptures are her work. The first public sculpture garden and currently the largest collection in the United States, the gardens include 1,200 pieces by 350 sculptors. Meandering through walkways of botanical displays interspersed with art, the experience is valued even by children and those who don't consider themselves as art connoisseurs. Visitors can sometimes even interact with resident sculptors and view work in progress. The Lowcountry Zoo is part of the garden experience. It houses domestic animals which would have been part of plantation life in this area in the 1800s. Native animals also live in a natural habitat, and birds live in an aviary which is built over a cypress swamp. Seasonal special events often add to the experience of the leisurely self-guided tour of the property. This is an experience which cannot be matched. *($)*

HOBCAW BARONY

(22 Hobcaw Rd., Georgetown ☎ 843.546.4623
🖱 hobcawbarony.org) Forestry and biology research are
conducted on this reserve of 17,500 acres of undeveloped
plantation property. It was part of the lowcountry's rice empire
until the turn of the 20th century. It was used as a winter
hunting retreat by the South Carolina millionaire Bernard M.
Baruch, who was noted for his Wall Street success and associa-
tion with international political leaders. The current outdoor
laboratory was created by Baruch's daughter who died in 1964.
Visitors are taken on tours by a van to the historic houses and
a slave village. One of the houses even allows admission for a
reasonable fee. Reservations are suggested. Frequent programs
and special activities are offered such as birding or fly fishing
adventures. The Discovery Center is open on weekdays all
year with free exhibits including Native American artifacts, rice
culture, and marine information. *($$)*

GREAT AMERICAN RIVERBOAT COMPANY

(8500 Enterprise Rd. ☎ 843.650.6600 🖱 mbriverboat.com)
Three separate departure sites for the different boats are the
best way to locate one of these scenic cruises on the Atlantic
Intracoastal Waterway and the Waccamaw River. The *Jungle
Princess* departs from the marina at Grand Dunes and cruises
round trip north to Barefoot Landing. The view is of upscale
homes along the water as well as some wildlife and scenic
water scapes with narration for 150 passengers. Dinner cruises
are scheduled as well as day trips. The *Jungle Baby* departs
from Waccatee Zoo with only six passengers and is more
likely to encounter views of alligators or other wildlife along
the river. The barracuda jet boat also leaves from the Grand

Dunes Marina with six passengers for a true speed tour of the waterway. All schedules and prices vary. *($$)*

MYRTLE BEACH SPEEDWAY

(🖱 **myrtlebeachspeedway.com**) Opened in 1958 west of the city, live stock-car racing is enjoyed by NASCAR fans every Saturday night. Several major racing events also take place during the year. Local divisions include the Mini Stock, Street Stock, Limited Late Models, Super Truck, and NASCAR Whelen All-American Series Late Model Stock Cars. General admission seating is $12 for adults. *($)*

NASCAR SPEEDPARK

(1820 21st Ave. N. Ext. ☎ 843.912.8725

🖱 **nascarspeedpark.com**) All types of rides for little or big kids or adults include themed or simulated race cars with indoor and outdoor tracks. Bumper boats, an arcade, and two NASCAR-themed miniature golf courses are also to be found here. It's open year-round except for an occasional holiday week, and hours vary widely during the seasons. Individual tickets are sold, although the best deal for race-car buffs is a day pass. Those interested in the water park and the pavilion park might opt for the three-park pass for the best package deal. Visitors on extended or repeat trips might consider an annual pass. *($$)*

MYRTLE BEACH PELICANS BASEBALL

(1251 21st Ave. N., BB&T Coastal Field ☎ 843.918.6000

🖱 **myrtlebeachpelicans.com**) Myrtle Beach lost its professional baseball team, the Myrtle Beach Hurricanes, in 1992. Due, in part, to the fact that the facilities they played in were not up to the standard that the parent team, the Toronto Blue Jays, expected. In 1998, the city of Myrtle Beach gave the go ahead to plan and build a new stadium for a farm team that would be of a major league team yet to be announced.

That team turned out to be the Atlanta Braves, and the new team in Myrtle Beach was named the Pelicans. The Pelicans took the field in the new stadium on 22nd Ave. N. nearly a decade ago. With many residents having followed the Atlanta Braves through Superstation TBS, it has been fabulous for all baseball fans along the Grand Strand and visitors who come to the beach to see the Braves' stars of tomorrow.

The Myrtle Beach Pelicans play in the Class A Carolina League, in existence for over 60 years. The league has a rich history of its own. The names that have gone through the Carolina League in those years sounds like the Who's Who in Major League Baseball. From Willie McCovey and Earl Weaver to Barry Bonds and Brian McCann, the Braves catcher in 2009, they all played ball in the Carolina League.

The Pelicans have seen many stars reach the parent club through the years. The arrival of the Pelicans in Myrtle Beach coincided with the Braves winning a record 14 consecutive division championships (1991-2005). There are many of the stars that were on those late 90's through 2005 Brave teams that got their feet wet in professional baseball as Pelicans. Included in that list are "Raffy" Furcal, Adam LaRoache, Jeff Franceour, and Marcus Giles.

The Pelicans stadium is ideally situated, right across the street from Broadway at the Beach. This park is a great location for fans to take in a game. Spectators can visit Broadway before the game, eat dinner, see the game, and then head back to Broadway for an after-game refreshment and snack. Although there is ample parking at the stadium, being across the street from Broadway also is convenient for the abundance of parking that is available there. *($$)*

RIPLEY'S AQUARIUM

(1110 Celebrity Cir., Broadway at the Beach ☎ 843.916.0888 🖱 myrtlebeach.ripleyaquariums.com) Interactive and living exhibits are presented for education and entertainment. It's one of the most visited attractions in the state. Gliding through the moving tunnel to watch divers feeding sharks or sometimes mermaids, and touching horseshoe crabs lend interest to this visit. Group visits are welcome. It's open every day of the year from 9:00 a.m. until 10:00 p.m. Single tickets are $3.99 for children ages two to five; $9.99 for ages to 11 and $18.99 for adults. Combination tickets are also available to include the other Ripley's attractions on Ocean Blvd.: **Moving Theatre, Believe It or Not Museum, Haunted Adventure or Marvelous Mirror Maze.** *($$)*

THE RIPKIN EXPERIENCE

(☎ 888.RIPKIN1 🖱 ripkintournaments.com) This is a world-class baseball complex offering scheduled week-long summer tournaments. With two regulation-sized and five youth fields designed after historic ballparks, the complex also offers spring training programs for high school and college baseball and softball teams. Family packages include lodging and vacation amenities combined with the baseball tournament experience. *Cost varies for special programs.*

AMUSEMENT PARKS

There are plenty of activities that families with young children can enjoy at Myrtle Beach. The area has a good variety of amusement parks that can keep kids and adults alike occupied.

FAMILY KINGDOM AMUSEMENT PARK

(300 S. Ocean Blvd. ☎ 843.626.3447 ⬤ family-kingdom.com)
This is the only amusement park on the oceanfront in Myrtle Beach. It's smaller than the Pavilion which was the dominant amusement for many years and was demolished in 2007. The wooden roller coaster and large Ferris wheel offer ocean views. From go karts to kiddie rides, midway games and funnel cake, it's all here. The amusement park season opens in early April and closes in late September. With no admission charge, the park charges per ride. The water park across the street opens in late May and closes in late August with day pass rates or combo rates for both parks. Hours vary. *($$)*

FREESTYLE MUSIC PARK

(2950 Backstage Blvd., U.S. 501 ☎ 843.236.7625
⬤ freestylemusicpark.com) The newest amusement park in Myrtle Beach, this park is the re-creation of Hard Rock Park which was only open for one season but closed down due to financial troubles. A wide variety of music can be heard throughout the park. Its unique quality lies in the different village concepts that have been incorporated in the rides, music, and food, ranging from country to British and other eclectic choices. Live music on outdoor stages, interactive children's activities, and fireworks can fill several hours for an active family. It opens in late May and closes in early September, with weekend hours only during the last few weeks.

Season passes, children's specials, and occasional military specials are available. *($$$)*

OCEAN DRIVE PAVILION AMUSEMENT PARK

(Ocean Blvd. at Main St., North Myrtle Beach

🖱 **northmyrtlebeachonline.com)** A collection of rides, relocated after several years in the Grand Prix spot, was placed in 2009 at the central beach access of North Myrtle Beach, known as the Horseshoe. A Ferris wheel, flying swings, carousel, Orient Express coaster, and several other rides and games add to the arcade and lend the nostalgia of the 1950s and 1960s beach era. Plans are for the park to be open from Memorial Day in late May until Labor Day in early September. Off season, it can't be spotted here. *($$)*

PAVILION NOSTALGIA PARK

(1171 Celebrity Sq., Broadway at the Beach ☎ 843.918.8725

🖱 **pavilionnostalgiapark.com)** This is a collection of rides which was moved from the pavilion amusement park on the boulevard after its demolition in 2007. The 1912-era carousel is a true piece of nostalgia for amusement lovers, but the long-standing tradition of the park was based on its location in addition to the rides. The majority of these rides are suitable for small children. Single ride tickets are sold, as are bundles of tickets or the three-park pass, which includes the water park and speedpark. *($$)*

STATE PARKS

Visitors looking to explore the natural surroundings of Myrtle Beach can head to one of the open spaces that offer opportunities for hiking, camping, and other activities like birding and viewing wildlife.

HUNTINGTON BEACH STATE PARK

(16148 Ocean Hwy., Murrells Inlet ☎ 843.237.9255 🖰 huntingtonbeachsc.org) This oceanfront park is across the highway from Brookgreen Gardens. It's a spectacular spot with a secluded three-mile beach, hiking trails, camping and fishing opportunities. The forested beach is bordered by freshwater lagoons and salt marsh where birding, wildlife, and botanical views are a special treat. Frequent park programs offer lecture and educational tours led by rangers, which often focus on birds, alligators, and other coastal wildlife. Hours vary during the year, and the fees range from $3 to $5 per person. See the "Lodging" chapter for details about camping here. ($)

MYRTLE BEACH STATE PARK

(4401 S. Kings Hwy. ☎ 843.238.5325 🖰 myrtlebeachstatepark.net) South Carolina's first state park opened here in 1935. It was a project of the Civilian Conservation Corps. It includes a campground in the oceanfront woods, picnic shelters, a fishing pier, and a wide beach. A nature center and educational programming provide engaging opportunities for families to learn about the environment and the natural resources of the area. The maritime forest has been declared a Heritage Trust Site. It's open daily from 6:00 a.m. until 8:00 p.m. or 10:00 p.m., depending on the time of year. Park admission is $4 per adult; $2.50 for South Carolina senior citizens; $1.50 for children between 5 and 15 years; free for children 5 and younger. See the "Lodging" chapter for details on staying at the park. ($)

MINIATURE GOLF

If golf along the Grand Strand is king then miniature golf along the Grand Strand is queen. There seems to be a miniature golf course on every block as one drives along U.S. 17. The old days of putting through windmills and up a steep incline are way in the past. The courses that are in the Myrtle Beach area are all theme oriented. That theme can be the jungle, a safari, a plane crashed into a mountain, or a lost treasure. Each course has its own theme.

Twelve miniature golf courses are located within Myrtle Beach plus 50 others throughout the area, hosting an estimated three million rounds of miniature golf each year. Two par three golf courses are also located in the city. A visitor will not need a map, directions, or reservations to happen upon a friendly course. See the "Golf" chapter for details and recommendations of full-size golf courses.

Attractions

MAYDAY GOLF

(715 U.S. 17 N., North Myrtle Beach ☎ 843.280.3535
☗ maydaygolf.com) As visitors drive into the parking lot of Mayday Golf, they may think they have happened upon a tragedy. All that is visible is an airplane that seems to have struck a mountain. As play begins, it becomes obvious that the pilot has landed the plane on top of a mountain and the passengers on board (the players) passed their time awaiting rescue by playing golf on this tropical island. Players climb Rescue Mountain and follow the path around Rescue Falls. *($)*

HAWAIIAN RUMBLE

(3210 U.S. 17 S., North Myrtle Beach ☎ 843.272.7812
☗ prominigilf.com) Hawaiian Rumble is probably the most famous miniature golf course along the Grand Strand. It has

been featured in numerous magazine articles. It was also the site of a climatic car wreck scene in the movie *Chasers* which was filmed here starring Dennis Hopper and Tom Berringer. In 2003, the Travel Channel chose it as one of their Top 10 Miniature Golf Courses in the U.S. It has also been the home of the Masters in miniature golf frequently played here in October.

The theme of Hawaiian Rumble is a gigantic volcano. As it erupts, unsuspecting drivers at a nearby stoplight invariably look around to see if they are about to drive into a catastrophe. Flames erupt from the top and players all gasp the first time they experience the eruption. The 40-foot volcano is the center of the miniature course. *($)*

RUNAWAY BAY

(1800 U.S. 17 S., Garden City ☎ 843.215.1038
⛶ tupelobay.com) Runaway Bay has two 18-hole courses for family fun. The theme at Runaway Bay is Jamaican. One course, Cockpit Country, is handicap accessible. The other 18-hole course is Dunns River Falls. Both courses have wonderful views of their 40-foot waterfalls. They also feature caves and tunnels which must be traversed for a good score. The airplane that sits in the middle of the pond on these courses is one of many highlights for family fun. *($)*

WINERIES

The vineyards of the Myrtle Beach area are a definite stopover for guests looking to indulge in some wine tastings and tours to learn about some of the wines indigenous to the region.

LA BELLE AMIE VINEYARD

(SC 90 at St. Joseph Rd., Little River ☎ 843.399.9463
🖱 labelleamie.com) The working vineyard sells a limited variety
of wines, the muscadine being made from the grapes grown
here and other wines being from family-run wineries in Europe
and distributed exclusively in this shop. Tastings are offered
Monday through Saturday at $5 for five samples. Frequent
festivals are hosted with emphasis on arts, crafts, and local
musicians combined with wine tastings. Tour groups are
welcomed for guided tours by the vineyard owner. Wine accessories, sauces, and salsas are sold in the gift shop. *($)*

SILVER COAST WINERY

(Barbecue Rd., Ocean Isle, NC ☎ 910.287.2800
🖱 silvercoastwinery.com) This working winery is about eight
miles north of the South Carolina border, but an easy drive for
an afternoon of wine-tasting or attending a festival. The muscadine grapes grown here are sometimes sold in a pick-your-own
fashion as well as used to produce some of the wines. The wines
have won dozens of international awards. Regional artists' paint-
ings and sculptures are featured in changing exhibits. *($)*

HYMAN VINEYARDS

(2980 S.C. 378, Conway ☎ 843.397.2100
🖱 hymanvineyards.com) Products are created from muscadine
grapes and red raspberries grown here. Grapes also can be
purchased here and you can even pick your own. The General
Store hosts wine tastings by appointment at $5 which includes
a logo wine glass. Several wine varieties are produced as well as
neutraceuticals and cosmaceuticals, all the result of extensive
research and combinations of natural fruits and vegetables
grown here at the family-owned farm vineyard. *($)*

Entertainment

At Myrtle Beach, there is no dearth of entertainment for diverse tastes. The entertainment includes professionally produced, high-quality shows with music as the central theme for most of them. Beginning in the late 1980s, theaters popped up to put the area on the entertainment map of the country. Some called it the country music capital of the south. Some referred to the Branson, Missouri phenomenon, where live entertainment was drawing tourists by the carload or busload. After several years, a few of these fell by the wayside, such as the theaters of Ronnie Milsap and the Gatlin Brothers. The major theaters remained while varying far from the country music theme and incorporating something for almost everyone.

High quality sound, lights, special effects, costuming, and staging support the serious talent of musicians, vocalists, dancers, and comedians who present the regular house shows. Nationally recognized performers are frequently presented at all of the venues.

January is the only month which is typically dark for some of the theaters, with possible exceptions of a couple of weekend specials. After the break, new or refreshed house shows roll out, and the remaining winter months are prime time for tour groups, meetings, and conventions to take advantage of superb entertainment when the lodging rates are at their lowest and traffic is at its slowest.

All theaters are handicap accessible, and parking is plentiful in the surrounding lots. There is enough space for dozens of tour buses. It's advisable to check with each venue for ticket information. Prices vary widely depending on the performance and season. All offer group rates, and some offer children's rates and varying specials for seasonal programs or for local attendance.

Watching a performance at one of the theaters listed is a must. Choose a different one which is most suitable for your party for each different visit.

ALABAMA THEATRE
(Barefoot Landing, U.S. 17 ☎ 843.272.2222
☎ alabama-theatre.com) The group began playing in 1970 at The Bowery in the center of Myrtle Beach's oceanfront boulevard area. They called their group Wild Country and played for tips only. The name "Alabama" came from a sign used as a backdrop on The Bowery's stage. They left Myrtle Beach for Nashville and a major record label contract. In 1993, the super successful group then named Alabama returned to their hometown roots and established their namesake theater where they played at least once each year when touring.

Country, Motown, and classic legendary acts each year include such recognized names as George Jones, Loretta Lynn, and Little Richard. Two signature shows are updated each year: *One The Show* and *The Christmas Show*. Much of the talent is local in each of the house shows, although auditions are conducted regularly with new performers added. The energetic dance and music of the house shows are top-of-the-line and applause-worthy. Special group rates, season tickets, and children's free tickets are offered. Backstage tours or educational tours are part of the group packages. Popcorn and refreshments are sold during intermission, but no alcoholic drinks.

THE CAROLINA OPRY

(8901A Bus. 17 N. ☎ 843.913.4000 🌐 thecarolinaopry.com)
This theater delivers high-energy music, comedy, and dance delighting visitors and locals. Calvin Gilmore created The Carolina Opry in 1987 as a venue for live country music. It was patterned loosely after the famed Grand Ole Opry and the Branson theaters. The Missouri native performs here on occasion and can also be seen frequently at the Grand Ole Opry in Nashville.

Today the theater continues to draw audiences to professionally produced live performances. Not all of it is country music. American popular music features almost every genre from the Beatles to beach music to the Motown sound. The second traditional show presented annually is the holiday program with warm classics for the season. A popular pianist showcased here for some Christmas seasons is Rocky Fretz who released a new album of his own original music in 2009.

A recent addition to the daytime program is a dazzling light show accompanied by some Pink Floyd tracks. Refreshments are sold with no alcoholic drinks.

DOLLY PARTON'S DIXIE STAMPEDE

(8901B Bus. 17 N. ☎ 843.497.9700 🌐 dixiestampede.com) This is a dinner show similar to Dolly Parton's theaters, which are also located in Branson and Pigeon Forge. The show includes dazzling lighting, music, and performance with trick horseback riding and sometimes buffalo or other live animals in special appearances. *Christmas in Dixie* is a warm traditional show with camels in a live nativity scene. The theater is popular with tour groups and children and suitable for any age or interest.

Group rates are offered and the theater also arranges private, themed events. The four-course dinner featuring Cornish hen, and served to guests during the performance, is an additional highlight of attending a show here. The vegetable soup is so popular that the mix is sold online. Vegetarian meals are available by request. No alcoholic drinks are served in this family style venue. Don't be surprised if waiters pass the hat for tips after the meal.

HOUSE OF BLUES ✪ Must See!
(4640 Hwy. 17 S., Barefoot Landing ☎ 843.272.3000
⦿ houseofblues.com) Built in 1997 with old tin salvaged from a rural tobacco barn, the restaurant and concert hall were designed to recreate a traditional farmhouse and tobacco warehouse.

The venue is home to a collection of eclectic folk art featuring such notables as Jimmy Lee Sudduth. Much of the art was created by self-taught African-Americans who created their art from mud, molasses, and a variety of discarded items. Some appear to be rants or a series of words painted or drawn on slabs of wood. Disparate drawings of Elvis, Jesus, Buddha and flowers, cats, and dogs might appear on the same wall. The entertainment value of the art is part of the charm of the concert hall.

Sunday Gospel brunch features a buffet and a hand-clapping musical extravaganza of live Southern gospel music, performed by African-American college choirs or soloists. With a slogan such as "Praise the Lord and pass the biscuits," the concept is clear.

Concerts feature such notables as B. B. King, Bonnie Raitt, Blues Traveler, and David Allan Coe among other stalwarts. An intriguing murder mystery dinner theater is also a frequent offer.

Free live entertainment for dancing and dining is presented during the summer in the restaurant or in the B B Blues Bar outdoors in a setting resembling a New Orleans blues joint. Corporate events and private functions are also welcomed.

The restaurant is located in an adjoining building to the concert hall. See the "Dining" chapter for details. House of Blues is a must see, whether choosing a concert, a cocktail, a meal, or just browsing the company store and getting a look at the overall venue.

IMAX DISCOVERY THEATER

(1195 Celebrity Cir., Broadway at the Beach., U.S. 17 S. ☎ **843.444.3333 ⊙ imax3dmyrtlebeach.com)** The only entertainment venue listed here which does not present live performances, the IMAX presents large format film on a screen that is six stories tall. Polarized 3D glasses are provided to the audience for the 3D films to produce the visual effect of high-resolution images. Educator's guides are provided for many of the shows. The programs are shorter length than typical movies, resembling documentaries rather than fictional stories, and the quality of production meets professional standards.

LEGENDS IN CONCERT

(301 Bus. 17 S., Surfside ☎ **843.238.7829** ⊙ **legendsinconcert.com)** Elvis Presley, the Blues Brothers, and Marilyn Monroe come to life daily in the tribute shows held in this theater. The performances are live, and the stunning look-alikes merit a double take when seen in celebrity appearances. The impersonators rotate among the various venues for this corporation including Atlantic City, Las Vegas, Branson, Seattle, Foxwoods, and Coushatta. Group rates are offered for these shows with a backdrop of state-of-the-art lighting, laser, and sound. The venue is smaller and older than other theaters and gives the feel of an intimate gathering.

MEDIEVAL TIMES

(2904 Fantasy Way, U.S. 501 ☎ 843.236.4635
🖱 medievaltimes.com) Royalty, knights, wenches, and serfs against a backdrop of a recreated 11th-century Spanish castle provide an entertaining dinner theater experience. The meal, to be eaten without utensils, includes tomato bisque soup, garlic bread, roasted chicken, share rib, potato, pastry, and beverages. A vegetarian meal is served on request. Mead is sold separately at the bar, but not included in the ticket price. The audience plays the role of guests invited to a festival with its accompanying tournament for entertainment. Jousting, swordsmanship, horsemanship, and hand-to-hand combat depict a story of Medieval Spain with audience teams encouraged to cheer their knights. Before the show, a tour of the medieval torture museum is offered. More than 400 horses used in the show's nine castles throughout the United States are raised on their farm in Texas where they breed the Spanish Andalusians. Group rates are offered, along with occasional free offers for kids and teenagers. The professional show is an exciting presentation enjoyable for any age.

PALACE THEATRE

(Broadway at the Beach, U.S. 17 S. ☎ 843.448.9224
🖱 palacetheatremyrtlebeach.com) Primary shows which rotate

here are *Le Grande Cirque* and *The Magical Spirit of Ireland*. A Christmas show is usually added for the holiday season. Le Grande Cirque includes clowns, jugglers, Russian trick poodles, fire eaters, dancing, and acrobatics performed to music on the big stage. Performers come from far and wide, including Europe, China, Russia, and Monte Carlo. *The Magical Spirit of Ireland* is presented in a small showroom and features Irish tenors and dancers.

THE SHAG

The shag is known as South Carolina's state dance. The dance originated in North Myrtle Beach and has evolved into a life-style and culture which reaches beyond the actual moves on the floor.

A dance resembling a medium-speed jitterbug with specific patterns in rhythm, the shag is performed to beach music. It's all about the steps, and spectators have their eyes riveted on the intricate foot movements. The male partner leads and typically showboats, while the female is expected to follow.

The term S.O.S., which means Society of Stranders, refers to events which are planned for three specific dates during each year and referred to as Spring Safari in April, Mid Winters in January, and Fall Migration in September. An annual July event is set for Junior S.O.S.

The Society of Stranders is a social membership organization, with social being the operative word. The events originated in 1980 with a spring S.O.S. Events now include contests, competitions, and sometimes live bands. Hundreds of dancers, usually baby boomers, give or take a few years, now frequent the area during these events, most centered in North Myrtle Beach.

From 1955 until 1994, The Pad was known as the center of the shagging community. A makeshift club, created under a second floor pad where lifeguards stayed, included a dance floor on the sand and typical surroundings suitable for a few beers and some heavy music and dancing.

Apart from the primary annual events, a few favorite clubs for shaggers fill the dance floors any time of year. Popular venues in North Myrtle Beach are **Ducks Beach Club, Fat Harold's Beach Club,** and **O D Pavilion**. Also, the Spanish Galleon is located in the **Ocean Drive Beach and Golf Resort** which houses the Shagger's Hall of Fame.

Classes are also offered in several clubs. The event dates skirt around other major events and peak seasons for family travel, so the dancers can comfortably fill their choice of hotels, rental houses, and condos in the North Myrtle Beach area. Workshops are scheduled during other time periods.

Shag: the Movie, released in 1989, was filmed in Myrtle Beach. The romantic comedy is the story of four young women in South Carolina in 1963.

Events

Festivals, exhibits, entertainment, and sports events are a big part of life along the South Carolina coast, especially during spring and fall which are ideal seasons for visitors to enjoy outdoor activities. Many visitors to Myrtle Beach choose their specific interest for a focal point in scheduling a trip. Several offer opportunities for vendors or for participation as well as for spectators. Food is the focus of many festivals, and they present prime opportunities for visitors to sample local fare whether from restaurants or street vendors. It's less expensive than choosing a meal in a restaurant when one wants to try something new. Weather is not a factor, as all typically continue rain or shine. Dates, prices, and some details may vary from year to year. The activities are generally similar and are scheduled during the same time period and same location each year. Many of the major events are free to the public.

SPRING EVENTS

The months of spring see Myrtle Beach playing host to several outdoor events. It is also the time of year when bikers descend here to participate in bike weeks. There is something for everybody with events ranging from an arts festival to a St. Patrick's Day celebration.

CAN AM DAYS

(☎ 843.626.7444 🖱 canamdays.com) Canadian American Days is an annual tradition sponsored by the Myrtle Beach Area Chamber of Commerce and typically scheduled for the second weekend in March. It is a city-wide welcome to

Canadian visitors who frequently arrive during this season. It usually includes a golf tournament and free concerts along with a cheer and dance competition for students. The opening of the festival and competitions are hosted at the Myrtle Beach Convention Center, and other activities may be set for various locations.

ST. PATRICK'S DAY FESTIVAL

(Main St., North Myrtle Beach ☎ 843.282.2662 🖱 nmbevents.com) This is a traditional street festival on the Saturday closest to St. Patrick's Day, usually the second Saturday in March, hosted by the North Myrtle Beach Chamber of Commerce. It involves a parade, live entertainment, and vendors selling green beer, other beverages, plenty of festival foods, arts, and crafts. Thousands of fun-loving visitors and locals are often attired in green or painted with shamrocks to claim some Irish heritage.

RIVERTOWN MUSIC AND ARTS FESTIVAL

(Downtown Conway ☎ 843.248.6260 🖱 conwayscchamber.com) Local artisans and restaurants treat visitors with background jazz and blues in the historic downtown of Conway. The annual free festival is produced by Conway Main Street the first Saturday in May.

TASTE! ✪ Must See!

(2101 N. Oak St. ☎ 843.333.7972 🖱 tasteshows.com) This is a new event set to begin in 2010, and planned as a continuing annual gourmet trade show and tasting expo. Celebrity chefs including Guy Fieri, Fabio Viviani and Aaron McCargo, Jr.

are expected to appear for demonstrations and book signings. Children aged four to 12 will be able to experience cooking workshops. Seminars, cooking competitions, along with luncheons, dinners, and wine tastings are scheduled for the Myrtle Beach Convention Center. It promises to be well worth a visit.

BIKE WEEKS

Each year, the Grand Strand is host to three motorcycle rallies. There are two Harley Davidson rallies, one in May and the other in late September and running into early October. Also in May is the **Black Biker/Atlantic Beach Bike Fest**.

Harley Davidson bikers start arriving in early May for a ten-day rally. Some arrive so early that many residents of the Grand Strand insist that it is really a two-week rally. This is by far the bigger of the two Harley Davidson rallies with more than 250,000 attendees.

The October Harley Davidson rally is not as old, nor is it as well-attended as the May rally, but the bikers are just as enthusiastic about being at the beach. There are many activities for the bikers to attend at bars and nightclubs during both rallies. Besides being able to rendezvous with other bikers, one of the most popular activities is to visit the various locations where venders set up shop in their tents and sell Harley Davidson and biker gear and accessories.

The Black Biker/Atlantic Beach Bike Fest is held each year during the Memorial Day weekend. Although this rally is sponsored by the town of Atlantic Beach, not enough hotels exist in this small town to accommodate the thousands of people

Events

who attend. Those attending have to find accommodations in the adjoining towns of Myrtle Beach, North Myrtle Beach and Little River, or other parts south. The fest is the largest activity each year in Atlantic Beach. It is a source of income for the small oceanfront town along the Grand Strand. Just as with the Harley Davidson Rallies, the Atlantic Beach Bike Fest excitement is in the meeting of old and new friends each year. There are also vendors in the town selling biker gear and accessories.

The area has been an old hand at hosting these rallies, with bikers, specifically Harley Davidson riders, coming to the beach to rally since the 1940s. However, in the last 15 years, all three rallies have grown to extraordinary proportions, so much so that it appears to have grown too much for the city of Myrtle Beach and some of the residents. After the 2008 May rallies, the city of Myrtle Beach passed laws that discourage bikers from coming into the city. Among these laws were a noise ordinance and the requirement that motorcycle riders wear helmets. Regardless, the bikers still come to the Grand Strand; however, a great proportion of them no longer stay within the city limits of Myrtle Beach.

Events

LITTLE RIVER BLUE CRAB FESTIVAL

(☎ 843.249.6604 📱 littleriverchamber.org) This is a huge festival in a tiny town. It's usually held in the middle weekend in May and is especially welcoming of bikers who are in the area for the annual Harley Davidson Motorcycle Rally. Food and beverage stalls stand alongside the craft and tee shirt stalls. Plenty of blue crab is available this time of year, but additional foods are equally popular. A 5K road race and a poker run are part of the event. Entertainment is often by the Coastline Band, the Fantastic Shakers, and the Castaways, or similar groups who are popular throughout the region. Admission fees and parking charge should be expected.

SUMMER EVENTS

Summer is a time for some fun in the sun, with arts events scheduled in parks and Independence Day festivities organized in various parts of Myrtle Beach.

SUN FUN FESTIVAL

(☎ 843.626.7444 ✆ visitmyrtlebeach.com) This is not a single event in one single location. It's the annual celebration of summer sponsored by the Myrtle Beach Area Chamber of Commerce opening the first weekend in June. It takes many forms with changes each year and is designed especially as free entertainment for summer family visitors. The Miss Sun Fun and Miss Sun Fun Teen pageants are part of the opening two days along with live entertainment and street fairs. The summer celebration officially ends with a Beach Boogie and Barbecue Festival on Labor Day Weekend.

ART IN THE PARK

(U.S. Bus. 17 at 16th Ave., N., Chapin Park ☎ 843.448.7690 ✆ wacg.org) Three art shows in the park are sponsored each summer by the Waccamaw Arts and Crafts Guild. Several dozen exhibitors showcase and sell everything from fine original watercolors, oils, and photographs to baskets, metal works, jewelry, painted or tie-dyed fabric, hats, scarves, and other novel creations each year. It's free to browse, and despite typically sultry days, it's an opportunity for planning gift giving and early holiday shopping.

RIVERFEST

(Downtown Conway ☎ 843.248.2273 🖱 conwayscchamber.com)
Two Saturdays before July 4 is the annual celebration of
Independence Day along the river in Conway. Live entertainment includes beach, boogie, and country. The business
expo, artisan market, bass fishing tournament, tennis classic,
raft race, food, fireworks, and activities for children are
added attractions.

FOURTH OF JULY

The fireworks displayed are spectacular for Independence
Day celebrations in several different locations. The beach is
the place to be, as fireworks in any section of sky can be seen
for many miles. North Myrtle Beach shows its patriotism at
the Cherry Grove Pier and Myrtle Beach shows are often at
Broadway at the Beach. Other fireworks' shows are common
during the summer as shopping and entertainment complexes
compete for weekly attention.

FALL EVENTS

The events during these months range from arts and crafts
festivals to an amateur golf tournament. There is even a
mini marathon organized to work up an appetite for the various food-centric events, including a festival centered around
Myrtle Beach's famous chicken bog.

CRAFTMEN'S CLASSICS ARTS AND CRAFTS FESTIVAL

**(2101 N. Oak St. ☎ 336.282.5550 🖱 gilmoreshows.com/
craftsmens_classics_myrtle_summer.shtml)** The first weekend
in August annually brings more than 250 crafters from

throughout the country to demonstrate and exhibit fine products in the Myrtle Beach Convention Center. It is consistently an award-winner for shows of its type. The three-day admission ticket is typically $7 for adults and $1 for children under 12. The free parking makes for a convenient and comfortable visit.

WORLD AMATEUR GOLF TOURNAMENT

(☎ 843.477.8833 🔱 worldamgolf.oom) It's the world's largest amateur handicap golf tournament. It's played throughout Myrtle Beach on as many as 50 courses over a four-day Labor Day weekend in early September. It is a large event, attracting 3,000 to 5,000 participants. The world's largest 19th hole follows each day's play with golf equipment and accessory exhibits, food, and beverage for all participants and guests at the Myrtle Beach Convention Center. This is a must play event for a golfer with a documented handicap.

SOUTH CAROLINA'S LARGEST GARAGE SALE

(2101 N. Oak St. ☎ 843.918.1235 🔱 cityofmyrtlebeach.com) The annual event sponsored by the city is usually set for the morning of the second Saturday in September. It attracts as many as 280 vendors to exhibit their wares in and around the Myrtle Beach Convention Center. Named after its original location, the event was held for many years on the five decks of the city's downtown parking garage. Thousands of shoppers and browsers attend and sometimes schedule a vacation especially for this unique event. Serious yard sale shoppers arrive early with rolling luggage or purchase the first tote bag offered to be prepared for gathering a large quantity of merchandise. Items typically include collectibles and antiques from furniture to silver as well as used clothing, books, jewelry, and retail overruns. No admission is charged to shoppers.

ATALAYA ARTS AND CRAFTS FESTIVAL
(**Huntington Beach State Park** ☎ 843.237.4440 🖱 scprt.com/ state-park-service/atalayafestivalartists) Usually set for the last September weekend, this arts and crafts event showcases an array of some 100 artists and crafters. The festival is one of the best of the year, with plenty of local food and beverage vendors and live music. The park setting itself is stunning with a forested beach, educational center, and wildlife-viewing areas. The festival is in and around the castle which was the winter home of sculptress Anna Hyatt and philanthropist Archer Huntington. The Huntington's **Brookgreen Garden** is located across the street from this property. A three-day event, the festival charges a daily admission, usually $6, or also offers a discounted, multi-day pass and free admission to children under 15 years. Parking is free with a festival ticket.

IRISH ITALIAN INTERNATIONAL FESTIVAL
(**Main St., North Myrtle Beach** ☎ 843.280.5570 🖱 afc.nmb. us/irishfestival.aspx?id=346) This festival sponsored by the city of North Myrtle Beach lasts an entire day, usually the last Saturday in September. The free street festival features themed live music and dance all day, several activities for children, art and craft exhibits, and all types of Irish and Italian food and drink. Friendly locals welcome visitors, and it's easy to enjoy fall weather when it's still hot but not as humid as mid-summer days. Free parking can be found along the city streets for several blocks surrounding the main festival area. Parking in hotel lots or garages should only be used by registered guests at those properties.

MYRTLE BEACH GREEK FESTIVAL

(3301 33rd Ave. N., St. John the Baptist Greek Orthodox Church ☎ 843.448. 3773 🖰 stjohn-mb.org/events/festival.htm) This four-day event is usually scheduled for the last weekend in September. The church grounds are filled with food and gift vendors with live music and space for children's activities and open folk dancing. The fellowship hall houses more food with tables and chairs for leisurely dining on homemade Greek foods. Gyro and baklava lovers find this the best opportunity for sampling and browsing. Church tours and free lectures about the Orthodox faith are scheduled several times each day. Admission is usually $1 for ages older than ten.

LITTLE RIVER SHRIMP AND JAZZ FEST

(☎ 843.249.6604 🖰 littleriverchamber.org) This is an annual two-day event on Columbus Day weekend. The waterfront streets of this little fishing village are filled with vendors selling a wide variety of handmade and commercial jewelry, pottery, art, and some oddities. The food is one of the highlights, although shrimp is no more prominent than crab cakes, oysters, and festival foods such as funnel cakes. Beer and wine are also sold, including some of the local product from nearby vineyards. The entertainment is enjoyable regional talent performing a variety of musical styles, strolling or in a tent with some seating. Visitors have to pay for both, parking and for festival admission. Walking shoes are needed as well as sunscreen if the temperature is still scorching, as the parking is likely to be several blocks from the festival entrance.

Events

MYRTLE BEACH MINI MARATHON WEEKEND

(☎ 800.733.7089 🖱 runmyrtlebeach.com) The inaugural event is set for 2010. Several thousand runners and walkers are expected to participate in this destination race for competitors throughout the United States. In addition to the 13.1-mile mini marathon, events include a health and fitness expo, a doggie dash, a high-heel run, and a 5K race. Some proceeds will go to The Grand Strand Humane Society. On the schedule are parties, a movie and much more to make for a fun-filled fall weekend. Registration and details are available online. This is a must for runners – and even amblers and strollers.

LORIS BOG-OFF FESTIVAL

(Loris ☎ 843.756.6030 🖱 lorischambersc.com) For 30 years, this small town has hosted a huge festival that lasts for a full week, and culminating on the third Saturday in October. It's centered around the chicken bog cooking contest and includes live music, children's activities, a parade, evening fireworks, and about 200 arts and crafts vendors. It's approximately 20 miles from the coast, and the festival provides a true look at traditional Southern small town activity.

WOODEN BOAT SHOW

(Front and Broad Sts., Georgetown ☎ 843.545.0015 🖱 woodenboatshow.com) Georgetown is less than an hour's drive from the center of Myrtle Beach, and easily accessible from the south end. The show is usually the third weekend in October and includes a national boat building challenge, wooden boat exhibits, and maritime arts and crafts with models on display. The boat building itself is a spectator event. As many as 20 two-man teams compete to build a modified version of a 12-foot Monhegan Skiff in less than four hours. Then a rowing relay race determines the seaworthiness of the vessels with judging on the speed of construction, quality of work, and rowing ability.

WINTER EVENTS

Winter is a time when visitors to Myrtle Beach can partake of Christmas celebrations beginning in November, attend a basketball tournament, or watch a Christmas Regatta among other events.

DICKENS CHRISTMAS SHOW & FESTIVALS WEEK
(2101 N. Oak St. ☎ 843.448.9483
🖱 dickenschristmasshow.com) The annual exhibition at the Myrtle Beach Convention Center held in the second weekend in November is a shopping extravaganza. Many visitors from surrounding counties and states kick off their holiday season among strolling minstrels and costumed vendors. Festivals of trees, wreaths, tables, and various competitions are included. Admission is usually $8 for adults, $4 for ages 2 to 12 with discounted multi-day passes and parking included.

SOUTH CAROLINA STATE BLUEGRASS FESTIVAL
(2101 N. Oak St. ☎ 706.864.7203 🖱 aandabluegrass.com/
Festivals/SouthCarolinaStateBluegra.html) Thanksgiving Day in late November is the traditional opening for a three-day festival with performances by top names in the bluegrass industry. The Myrtle Beach Convention Center is the site where six groups or more begin at noon each day and continue until 10:00 p.m. Ticket prices vary.

INTRACOASTAL CHRISTMAS REGATTA

(Little River to North Myrtle Beach ☎ 843.249.8888
☗ **christmasregatta.com)** The boat parade was founded in 1984
and is always held on the Saturday following Thanksgiving.
Visitors often choose this holiday weekend for a family gathering
at the beach. Small and large vessels are lit and decorated, while
families and revelers on the banks and onboard the boats kick off
the winter holiday season. The regatta begins at dusk from the
Little River Inlet, with viewing spots anywhere along the route,
and terminates at the Dock Holidays Marina in North Myrtle
Beach. Toys for underprivileged children and pet items for shelter
animals are collected at several spots during the boat parade.
Santa's Angels is a volunteer committee which manages the parade
and the associated fundraising and toy drives.

BEACH BALL CLASSIC

(2101 N. Oak St. ☎ 843.213.0032 ☗ beachballclassic.com)
This classic goes on for ten days during late December and
includes a 16-team national tournament, for both girls' and
boys' high school basketball, plus a Carolina Challenge with
a college women's game. Since 1991, it has grown into an
important event for visiting players and their families, as well
as any basketball loving spectators. Parking is plentiful and free
for the games at the Myrtle Beach Convention Center. Ticket
prices vary.

MYRTLE BEACH MARATHON

(☎ 843.293.7223 ☗ mbmarathon.com) A 5K, family fun run,
bicycle ride, and half marathon are included, with the marathon event held in the second or third weekend of February
annually. All parts of the event are located within the central

section of the city except for the adult post race party which is sometimes at **House of Blues** in North Myrtle Beach. Advance registration is required, and limits are set for numbers to participate in each event for safety reasons. It was established as a green event last year. This is a well organized and fun event, a must for a runner.

Sidewalk displays and window banners of beach stores often have advertisements claiming that they are "going out for business," the key word being "for," not that they are going out "of" business!

Shopping

Shopping in Myrtle Beach is geared toward families and discount hunting. The major outlet malls include nationally recognized names and outlet prices. The bargain shopping is so popular among European visitors in particular, that luggage is a frequent purchase for transporting the loot home. Items such as jeans, shoes and school clothing are plentiful and attract visitors to the area for regular shopping sprees. The state of South Carolina declares a tax-free shopping weekend, usually twice a year, when school-related products can be purchased with the incentive of saving a few dollars. Residents of neighboring states plan visits to the outlet malls, especially when gearing up a family for a school year.

General retail malls are anchored by such major regional chains as Belk. A few specialty boutiques and custom shops for men's and women's clothing do exist, but fashion shopping is scarce. Locals generally travel to Atlanta, New York or London for up-scale shopping.

Golfers, on the other hand, will find all well-known brand names here, as well as specialized shops including custom club-fitting, shoes, clothing, and accessories for men and women. All golf courses also have attractive golf shops with most of the expected brands of merchandise.

Beach stores are literally everywhere with a dozen different names. They can't be missed. They're big and bold and this is reflected in the tee shirts, bathing suits, beach toys, and souvenir items that they stock. Sidewalk displays and window banners often reel in bargain-hunters with advertisements claiming that they are "going out for business." The key word is for, not that they are going out of business – a slight distinction. The much-advertised hermit crab, usually free with purchase of cage, is sure to attract children and lure unsuspecting parents to these stores.

MALLS

Visitors to Myrtle Beach have a wide variety of malls that they can visit, with several nationally recognized malls established here.

COASTAL GRAND MALL
(U.S. 17 Bypass at U.S. 501 ☎ 843.839.9100
☙ coastalgrand.com) Major stores include Belk, Dillards, JC Penney, Sears, Dick's Sporting Goods, Old Navy, Books A Million, and Bed, Bath & Beyond. Entertainment, home furnishings, jewelry, health and beauty products, and all variety of apparel and footwear can be found here. A total of 170 stores are housed within the enclosed mall. Small shops, specialty boutiques, and fast-food storefronts are subject to change. A Cinemark theater includes eight screens. There is a restaurant district that is adjacent to the mall where the restaurants are primarily family-oriented, casual eateries which are chains. Though not itemized in the "Dining" chapter, they are easy to find during a shopping trip.

MYRTLE BEACH MALL
(10177 N. Kings Hwy. ☎ 843.272.4040
☙ shopmyrtlebeachmall.com) This mall has undergone a couple of name changes. First opened as Briarcliffe Mall, it was renamed Colonial Mall a few years ago. Subsequently,

with changes in ownership, and the demolition of the Myrtle Beach Mall in central Myrtle Beach, this mall on the far north border of Myrtle Beach was renamed and updated. Exhibits and activities such as health screenings are frequently hosted in the common areas within this enclosed mall. Currently this mall includes fewer than half of the number of stores which are found in the newer and larger **Coastal Grand**. The major stores are Books-A-Million and Belk which has a separate store for men and for women. A major feature at this location is the Bass Pro Shop which is the only one in the area and occupies an area almost as large as five football fields. It includes a huge fish tank with live specimen. Displays of apparel and equipment run the gamut from camping needs to golf, fishing, and almost any outdoor activity. Sports enthusiasts can lose themselves for many hours in this shop, and browsers who are not sports oriented can be entertained with the attractive exhibits and frequent activities underway. Restaurants within the mall, although with exterior entrances, are Islamorada Fish Company Restaurant and Ruby Tuesday, the only branch of each within this area. The Colonial Theater with 12 screens is located here.

TANGER OUTLET MALL, U.S. 501

(**U.S. 501** ☎ **843.236.5100** 🖱 **tangeroutlet.com**) More than 100 brands are featured in the outlet stores. Accessories, apparel, footwear, children's shops, and a few restaurants are located here. One major store which is only located here is the Cole Hahn Factory Outlet.

TANGER OUTLET MALL, KINGS ROAD

(**10835 Kings Rd., U.S. 17** ☎ **843.449.0491** 🖱 **tangeroutlet.com**) This outlet also houses more than 100 labels. Both of the

Tanger outlets include the major apparel and footwear stores such as Nike, Polo Ralph Lauren, Liz Claiborne, Kenneth Cole, Coach, Timberland, Wilson's Leather, and Bass. Anne Klein and Ann Taylor both are located in this mall and are not in the Hwy. 501 center.

SHOPPING, DINING, AND ENTERTAINMENT COMPLEXES

There are several places in Myrtle Beach where visitors can shop, dine, and indulge in some entertainment all at one location.

BAREFOOT LANDING ✪ Must See!

(4898 Hwy 17 S., North Myrtle Beach ☎ 843.272.8349 ☏ bflanding.com) This is a shopping, dining and entertainment complex located along the Intracoastal Waterway. Bridges across the marsh and ponds lead visitors throughout the sections amidst displays of shorebirds and turtles with an occasional alligator sliding through the water. More than 100 specialty and retail shops display a variety of toys, jewelry, souvenirs, and apparel.

Most of the restaurants, usually numbering between 12 or 14, are on the water. Choices range from steaks and seafood to pizza, hotdogs, and ice cream. See the "Dining" chapter for descriptions of recommended restaurants.

Entertainment is featured regularly at the **House of Blues** and nightly at **Alabama Theatre,** which are within the complex. See the "Entertainment" chapter for contact information and descriptions of theater and concert hall.

Attractions within the complex are **Alligator Adventure** and a number of other smaller but interesting choices such as ghost walks and tiger exhibits. See the "Attractions" chapter for further details.

The barefoot carousel is a free ride enticing to children. Adults will recognize the authentic replica of a Barnum & Bailey carousel with 41 animals cast from original molds.

Parking is plentiful, with outdoor scenic walks between the shops, restaurants, or theaters. Fireworks typically entertain visitors weekly on Monday nights during the summer. Special events such as classic car shows or motorcycle exhibits are frequently hosted in the parking lots. It's a must, whether for shopping, dining, entertainment, or a nice amble.

BROADWAY AT THE BEACH ✪ Must See!
(U.S. 17 at 21st Ave. N. ☎ 843.386.4662
⬤ **broadwayatthebeach.com)** This is another complex inviting the visitor to eat and drink in stylish surroundings. More than 100 specialty shops, 20 restaurants, 11 nightclubs, a theater, three hotels and even attraction rides for children, are laid out around a 23-acre manmade lake. The architecture of this development features separate villages. The New England, Caribbean, Charleston, and Heroes' Harbor each house different kinds of shops with gifts and specialty items.

The **IMAX Theater** and the Carmike's Broadway Cinema 16 offer entertainment on plenty of screens. Kiddie Rides and Nostalgia Park offer some of the attractions for children that were found at the old Pavilion on the Boulevard, a traditional Myrtle Beach attraction which was demolished in 2007. **Ripley's Aquarium**, the **Palace Theatre,** and **Coastal**

Federal Field are part of the complex. **Myrtle Waves Water Park** is across the street but is considered as part of the center. Exhibits and competitions such as a barbecue cook-off frequently are hosted in this center.

The nightlife based at Celebrity Square provides the safest spot for drinking and dancing the night away with as many as a dozen clubs and restaurants within walking distance, and taxi or shuttle transportation easily available to return partying guests to their hotels. See the "Dining" chapter for descriptions of recommended restaurants, and the "Attractions" chapter for information about the aquarium, the water park, the baseball complex and the pavilion. It's a must for the variety of browsing.

THE MARKET COMMON ✪ Must See!
(4017 Deville St. ☎ 843.839.3500 🖱 marketcommonmb.com)
The newest shopping complex in the area is the most upscale within an urban village community complex. Walking neighborhoods, ball parks, live-work housing and office units, plus vacation units are distinctive in this attractive area. Two dozen unique shops and 12 restaurants attract locals as well as visitors. See the "Dining" chapter for descriptions of recommended choices. Apart from plenty of choices for shopping and dining, there are frequent outdoor events scheduled, which visitors can attend for free.

SPECIALTY SHOPPING

For visitors looking for one-of-a-kind items that are specific to the region, listed below are some recommended shops worth visiting.

MARTINS PGA TOUR SUPERSTORE

(2310 Hwy. 17 S., North Myrtle Beach ☎ 843.272.6030 and 1400 29th Ave., Myrtle Beach ☎ 843.839.4653 📱 pgatoursuperstore.com) This well-known golf and sports specialty store has four locations in the area. It was begun by Martin, and when sold, carried the familiar name and retained the loyalty of most golf and other sports enthusiasts.

THE HAMMOCK SHOPS

(U.S. 17, Pawleys Island 📱 thehammockshops.com) This little village among the oak trees originated in 1938. With more than 20 small local shops and restaurants located here now, it is one of the interesting spots on the south end of the strand for finding unique gifts or such specialty items as the original Pawleys Island rope hammock. The center is open from 10:00 a.m. until 6:00 p.m. from Monday to Saturday. On Sundays, it opens at 1:00 p.m.

MYRTLE BEACH FLEA MARKET

(3820 S. Kings. Hwy. ☎ 843.477.1550 📱 myrtlebeachfleamarket.net) This is a collection of indoor vendor stalls in five connecting buildings which are air conditioned and heated. It's owned by a national company which also manages recognized markets in Phoenix and Memphis. It opens Thursday through Sunday year-round and daily from June through August. The eclectic combination of merchandise ranges from junk to antiques to clothing and used books. It's worth a visit on a rainy day or by guests planning a long visit and staying on the south end of the beach.

NORTH MYRTLE BEACH FLEA MARKET

(U.S. Hwy. 17 N., Little River ☎ 843.249.4701

🖱 nmbfleamarket.com) This flea market has an aggregate of nearly 350 indoor and outdoor shops and stalls, mainly in covered sheds. Only a couple of shops are air conditioned or heated. A wide variety of products can be found here including fresh vegetables and fruits as well as books, clothing, tools, jewelry, and other miscellaneous merchandise and junk, all of which changes routinely. It's a good place to head to for fresh produce, especially for visitors in the north part of the beach. The market stays open Friday through Sunday year-round.

Golf

The fact that the most popular attraction in the Myrtle Beach area by far is the 60 miles of beautiful beach is undisputed. During the summer months, this is the main draw for the area. Families from all over the east coast and Midwest flock here to enjoy their time in the sun. However, during the late and early winter, spring, and fall, a different type of visitor migrates to the area in large numbers. They come for only one reason. They take advantage of the plethora of golf courses that have made the Grand Strand somewhat of a golfing Mecca, especially recognized as such by those on the east coast, Midwest and Canada.

At the end of the 20th century, the area had more than 110 golf courses. This was truly the height of the golf tourism industry in the Myrtle Beach area. However, in the early 2000s, the land and housing boom exploded on the Grand Strand as retirees from all over the northeast and mid-Atlantic began to settle here for the mild winters and the golf courses. It soon became clear to many golf course owners that their land was worth much more as home sites than as 18 holes of par threes, fours, and fives. Thus many courses closed and became developments. Unfortunate as it was to see some of the area's courses bite the dust, it raised the quality of golf along the Strand. What remained was the best of the best that Myrtle Beach had to offer golfers. Today, almost all of the courses located along the Strand, approximately 73, are considered premium courses. With fewer courses, those course owners who had not upgraded their track in years had to bring theirs up to par, literally, to stay in business.

Coming to Myrtle Beach and playing golf is an annual ritual for many groups. For many who come in the late winter or early spring, it is a time for them to get their game in shape for the summer. For those who come in the fall and early winter, it is the last time they will probably pick up a club for several months. For both groups, it is a time that they savor.

Pricing a round of golf in Myrtle Beach can be a challenge in itself. If playing one of the premium courses, a golfer can certainly expect to pay more. Additionally, rates are increased during the period which the course owners consider prime time. In the spring and fall, all courses, whether premium or not, are going to be charging more. Prices usually change from winter rates to spring rates around the middle of March. Fall rates usually kick in around the latter part of September or early October. Of course, during winter, one can expect to pay less than any time of year. Summer rates are not significantly lower than spring and fall rates.

The grass on the courses also makes a significant impact on your choice of course. There are many strains of grass being developed all the time for courses. Such is the case at Barefoot Resort courses. Greg Norman Turf has come up with a grass type called GN-1, and it is on all the courses at Barefoot. The ones that most golfers know about however are two: Bent and Bermuda grasses. Most courses in Myrtle Beach have one or the other of these kinds of grass or some off shoot of them.

So what is the difference? It depends on your location. Bent-grass is a hearty grass that can stand the hard winters of the North. Bermuda, as one could guess by its name, is better in the South where the summers are much hotter. Myrtle Beach winter nights can be cold on occasion, and the summers are hot. So when playing golf along the Grand Strand, players can expect to play on some strain of either or both of these grass varieties during the rounds.

Going hand-in-hand with the pricing and the grass on the course is aerating the course. If the course is to be in good condition the majority of the time, work has to be done on it. Aerating is one of the maintenance jobs that must be done during specific times of the year. Many of the courses will tell the golfer when the tee time is being made whether the course is being aerated; however, some don't. When calling to make a time, especially during the fall, ask if aerating is being done. If it is underway, a discount round may be given, or a different course can be selected.

CENTRAL MYRTLE BEACH GOLF COURSES

The city limits of Myrtle Beach are considered the central section. If accommodations are in the central section, these golf courses are easily accessible with a minimum of driving time.

ARCADIAN SHORES GOLF CLUB

(701 Hilton Rd. ☎ 843.449.5217 ⛳ mbn.com) This course has had plenty of play and been one of the most popular courses since it opened in 1974. Reese Jones designed this track that has some 64 sand traps placed throughout the course. The lakes, trees, and elevated greens along with the sand make Arcadian Shores quite a challenge for even the seasoned player. Although the fairways are wide, shots must be strategic. This is a fine course to play. The local newspaper, *The Sun News*, as part of its golf compilation chose Numbers 2 and 13 as part of its Dream 18. The panel that put together this Dream 18 is a group of local experts verifying that this is a course the locals love.

DUNES GOLF AND BEACH CLUB

(9000 N. Ocean Blvd. ☎ 843.449.5914 🖰 dunesclub.net) The Dunes Golf and Beach Club, one of the oldest courses in the Myrtle Beach area, was designed by the fabled Robert Trent Jones in 1948. It is one of the few private courses in Myrtle Beach. Several of the major hotels are members, and players with accommodations at a member property are welcomed. The Dunes Club has consistently been ranked by every golf publication and is known as one of the best courses in America. Number 13, named "Waterloo" was named by *Sports Illustrated* as one of the best holes in the U.S. It has also been the site of many PGA events and qualifying tournaments. The course sits oceanfront and on many holes the golfer will either tee off or putt out with views of the Atlantic Ocean. It goes without saying that ocean winds affect the shots. The Dunes has Bentgrass and is always in superior shape.

PINE LAKES COUNTRY CLUB ✪ Must See!

(5603 Granddaddy Dr. ☎ 843.315.7700 🖰 pinelakes.com) Known around the golfing world as "The Grandaddy," Pine Lakes is a playing experience that must be taken advantage of if possible. It's even more important since the course is open after being closed for two years for renovations. It is in top form and still retains its Scottish theme. The renovations retained the Scottish golf experience.

Pine Lakes was the first course built in Myrtle Beach in 1927. The course is so historic that it is on the National Register

Golf

of Historical Places. One historic event that occurred at the club in 1954 was when Henry Booth Luce and other *Time-Life* executives conceived the idea for *Sports Illustrated* while at the club for a golf outing.

It was designed by St. Andrews native, Robert White. He just happened to become the first president of the PGA along with several other firsts and honors. During the renovations, SeaDwarf Paspalum grass was put down on the first course in the area to have such grass. It's a course that should be played at least once, if only for its historical value.

GRANDE DUNES GOLF CLUB

(8700 Golf Village Ln. ☎ 843.315.0333 ☗ grandedunes.com) The Intracoastal Waterway must be crossed to get to The Grand Dunes Resort Golf Club. This will not be your first view of the waterway because seven of the 18 holes are along the Intracoastal. Designed by Roger Rulewich, this course is ideal for golfers at any level. The six sets of tees see to that. The course was named one of the Top Ten New Courses when it opened in 2002. In 2007, *Golf Week* named Grande Dunes Resort course as the "Best Course You Can Play." The wide fairways are made of Bermuda, and putts roll across Bentgrass.

Although technically a public course, The Grande Dunes Resort Course has the feel of a private club. The course is always in great shape. The clubhouse has wonderful dining, and the pro rates second to none.

KINGS NORTH AT MYRTLE BEACH NATIONAL

(4900 National Dr. ☎ 843.235.6061 ☗ mbn.com) Kings North has been a staple for true golfers who visit Myrtle Beach since it opened in 1996. It has constantly been on all the lists of best-playing locations in Myrtle Beach and in America. Kings North is an Arnold Palmer signature course that has Bentgrass.

There are many great holes at this course; however, King's North is known for its signature hole "The Gambler." A par 5, it is a gamble to go for it by making an accurate shot count to an island fairway. Most golfers do gamble of course, but the smart shot may be to go around it. Number 12 is another hole on the course that sports an island. However this is an island green on this par 3.

Plenty of sand and water on this course challenge any golfer, but playing it makes one feel a little closer to Arnie. After the round, a visit to the Arnold Palmer Room in the clubhouse showcases some of his memories and memorabilia shared with golfers.

THE LEGENDS

(1500 Legends Dr. ☎ 843.236.9318 ☗ legendsgolf.com) The Legends has three excellent courses at this location. It is a full-facility golf resort, conveniently located off U.S. 501 S at the entrance to Myrtle Beach. The three courses are distinctly different from each other: Moorland, Heathland, and Parkland. At the Legends is one of the best practice areas that can be found anywhere.

If staying at the Legends Resort, be sure to stub out all cigarettes while entering, as it is a smoke-free zone. This includes the club-house, the resort building, and the Ailisa Pub. Smoking is allowed on the grounds of the resort and in some designated villas.

Golf

The Moorland Course was recently designated by *Golf Digest* as one of the 50 Toughest Courses in America. Enough said. Designed by Pete Dye, one can only assume he designed this course for mainly scratch or near-scratch golfers. If you are not one of these don't frustrate yourself and slow everyone else down. Stay away from it.

The Heathland Course was designed by Tom Doak in 1990, along the lines of the old links courses of the British Isles, including The Old Course at St. Andrews. It is, as a result, not the typical Myrtle Beach course with tree-lined fairways. Doak placed strategic bunkers to make up for the lack of trees.

The Parkland Course, also designed by Pete Dye, is more in line with what Myrtle Beach golf is all about: tree lined fairways and green side bunkers. Added to this are multi-leveled and undulating greens. This course takes advantage of the natural areas and terrain.

INTERNATIONAL WORLD TOUR GOLF LINKS
(2000 World Tour Dr. ☎ 843.236.2000 ☏ theworldtourgolf.com)
Never been lucky enough to travel and play some of the great courses around the world like Augusta National or St. Andrews, Bayhill, or Sawgrass? Then the trip to Myrtle Beach may be your best chance. This is truly an inspirational course. It has three nine-hole courses: The Championship, The Open, and The International. As one can imagine, this was no small endeavor by owner Mel Graham, who had to have over one million cubic yards of dirt moved to recreate these historic holes.

One of the fantastic treats is to play "Amen Corner" Numbers 11, 12, and 13 from Augusta National. This is after playing a replica of the par 3 Number 8 at Troon. All of these are on the Championship nine. The Open nine replicates Number 1 at St. Andrews, Number 16 at Pinehurst 2, and the famous island green at Sawgrass Number 17. The International nine has holes that could make a golfer swear that he is at Valderrama in Spain, or Inverness in Ohio.

Dress code is a must here at the International World Tour. Jeans are not allowed, whether they are short or long. Bermuda shorts are acceptable and only collared shirts.

NORTH STRAND GOLF COURSES

North Strand courses are within the areas of North Myrtle Beach; Little River; Brunswick County, NC and U.S. 9. If accommodations are in North Myrtle Beach, all of these courses are easily accessible with a minimum of driving time.

ABERDEEN COUNTRY CLUB

(701 Buck Trail, S.C. 9, Longs ☎ 843.399.2660 🖱 mbn.com)

Only a short drive from North Myrtle Beach on what the locals call Number 9, Aberdeen Country Club offers three nine-hole courses designed by Tom Jackson. They include the Highlands, Woodlands, and the Meadow. So if the regular 18 holes is not enough for the group, the other nine will suffice. This course has plenty of water to shoot over and an abundance of nature to enjoy along with golf. Almost all the holes on the three nines are trickier that they seem at first. Over the years this course has won awards from many publications including *Golf Digest.*

On some holes homes and condos line the fairway and surround the greens, so this can be somewhat confining to the player. Thus, it's suggested to be careful with language and behavior.

BLACK BEAR GOLF CLUB

(2850 S.C. 9, Longs ☎ 843.756.0550 📱 classicgolfgroup.com)
This course is just a short ride past the Intracoastal Waterway. This Tom Jackson-designed course was built in 1990 and has plenty of water hazards, with 23 lakes and more than enough sand to test one's abilities. This can be a very rewarding and fun golf course if the golfer picks the right tees to play. Expect to use almost all of the clubs in the bag. Black Bear can best be described as just a fun day of golf on a really nice course for all levels of play. However, for the high handicap player, this is especially a good course.

HEATHER GLEN GOLF LINKS

(U.S. 17, Little River ☎ 843.249.9000 📱 glensgolfgroup.com)
Heather Glen has three nine-hole courses and in 1987 was named the Best New Public Course in America. After some aging and maturing, the course is still fantastic, being honored in 2002 with four and one-half stars by the *Golf Digest* Readers Poll on "places to play." The courses were designed by Willard Byrd and Clyde Johnson. Heather Glen has a distinct Scottish flavor as evidenced by the name, the pot bunkers, and the waste areas that can be treacherous. Although there is some water, with lakes and streams on the course, water is not in over abundance at Heather Glen. Carved out of the forest in Little River, this course is really enjoyable to play.

Golf

THE LONG BAY CLUB

(843 S.C. 9, Longs ☎ 843.399.2222 📱 mbn.com) When riding by the Long Bay Club, a golfer can recognize the Jack Nicklaus-designed course. The mounds that have become his trademark are everywhere on this course, not to mention waste area traps. The waste area on number 10 has become famous to all golfers. This waste area trap encircles almost all of the fairway and green. This course has everything that challenges a golfer, including an island green. Long Bay can be very demanding and a challenge for the golfer with a high handicap, but this is one of the few Jack Nicklaus signature courses that is open to the public to play, so this is an opportunity definitely worth grabbing with both hands!

TIDEWATER GOLF CLUB AND PLANTATION

(1400 Tidewater Dr., North Myrtle Beach ☎ 843.249.3829 📱 tidewatergolf.com) In 1990, Tidewater Golf Club and Plantation was named the top new course by both *Golf Magazine* and *Golf Digest*. Nearly 20 years on, the Ken Tomlinson-designed, 18-hole course is still garnering accolades, as evidenced by being named one of the "Top 100 Greatest Public Courses" by *Golf Digest* for 2009-2010. Tidewater has become known in some circles as the Pebble Beach of the East.

This course has it all. While playing Tidewater it's easy to become somewhat distracted by the surrounding views. These include the Atlantic Ocean, the Intracoastal Waterway, and the saltwater marshes of Cherry Grove Beach Inlet. The cart path winds through forests that contain live oaks, streams, and lakes. This course will challenge a player with wind, elevation changes and distance. Course management is a must at Tidewater Golf

Golf

Course. It is a tough course by any standard, so the golfer must be up for a challenge to enjoy Tidewater.

GLEN DORNOCH

(4840 Glen Dornoch Way, Little River ☎ 843.249.2541
☗ **glensgolfgroup.com)** The sister course to Heather Glen Golf Course and almost directly across the highway is Glen Dornoch Golf Club. Clyde Johnston designed this beautifully laid out course, which opened in 1996 to rave reviews. It is still getting those reviews today, being named one of the top courses in South Carolina by the 2009 SC Golf Rating Panel. A beautiful forest and wonderful views of the Intracoastal Waterway make this course stunning just to ride in the cart and enjoy. However playing it is an experience that will not soon be forgotten. Each shot must be thought about and calculated. Finishing up on number 18, which runs alongside the Intracoastal, is a fabulous way to end a day of golf.

BAREFOOT RESORT & GOLF

(4980 Barefoot Resort Ridge Rd., North Myrtle Beach
☎ **843.390.3200** ☗ **barefootgolf.com)** Barefoot Resort and Golf offers four courses. Each course is named for its course designer: Greg Norman, Davis Love III, Tom Fazio, and Pete Dye. This resort and golf club offers a top-of-the-line golfing experience. Whether the golfer is a weekend player or someone with a low handicap, Barefoot Resort offers a pleasurable round of golf. On all of the courses, the fairway grass is GN-1, which is a hybrid turf developed for and by Greg Norman Turf. While each course is unique in its own way, as per designer, each of the holes reflects and enhances the native plant life and nature of coastal South Carolina.

Golf

The Love course is just plain fun to play. It is ranked as number one by *Golf Digest* of all the Myrtle Beach courses. It has a beautiful setting and has even recreated the ruins of an antebellum plantation that could come into play for errant shots.

The Fazio Course has been honored numerous times since it was built. The latest is to be listed in the top 100 Golf Courses in America by *Golf Digest*. As always, Fazio uses the environment and the lay of the land to fashion a really nice course.

Pete Dye lives up to his reputation on The Dye course, and simply put, that means that this course is challenging. So come prepared, you may be humbled. The Dye Course hosts the annual Hootie and the Blowfish Monday after the Masters Pro-Am. This is a chance to see PGA stars, musicians, and actors take to the links and strut their stuff.

CROW CREEK GOLF CLUB

(245 Hickman Rd., NW of U.S. 17, Calabash ☎ 910.287.3081 ✆ crowcreek.com) Crow Creek Golf Club is just some two miles north of the South Carolina/North Carolina border, and is worth the drive. The course opened in 2000, and quickly became a favorite of the locals and tourists alike. Designed by Rick Robbins, the course is a pleasure to play. Most of the Tifsport Bermuda fairways are wide and somewhat forgiving. The Bentgrass greens make for a very enjoyable round of golf for all levels of skill. The golf course was carved from a 500-acre farm owned by the McLamb family. The family's cabin still stands beside the par 3 Number 8. It reminds golfers of what an old North Carolina fish camp was like back in the day.

Golf

OCEAN RIDGE PLANTATION

(351 Ocean Ridge Pkwy., Sunset Beach ☎ 843.448.5566, 910.287.1717 🖱 big-cats.com) Ocean Ridge Plantation is also known in the area as the Big Cats. Rightfully so, since the cats naming the courses are Lion's Paw, Panthers Run, Tigers Eye, and Leopard's Chase. These four cats are some of the nicest courses that can be played while in the Myrtle Beach area. Although they actually are in North Carolina, they are just a 20-minute drive up U.S. 17 N from North Myrtle Beach. Lion's Paw was designed by William Byrd, and the other three cats were designed by Tim Cate. They have all been awarded some honor over the years. Lion's Paw was given four stars by *Golf Digest*. Tigers Eye has been honored as one of "America's 100 Greatest Courses." In 2007, Leopard's Chase opened to much talk which has not stopped about what a course it is. If a stay in Myrtle Beach is not long enough to play all four, make sure that at least one of these makes the list to play and tame.

SHAFTSBURY GOLF AND FISH CLUB

(681 Cains Landing, Off S.C. 905 ☎ 843.369.0079 🖱 glensgolfgroup.com) Shaftsbury Glen is part of the Glens Golf Group, along with Glen Dornoch, Heather Glen, and Possum Trot. Playing this course can only be described as a challenge. Designed by Clyde Johnston with Winged Foot in mind, Shaftsbury Glen is slightly out of the way off S.C. 905 near Conway, but worth the distance with some fantastic golf on offer. This course is in a rural setting, with homes around the course.

The smooth and fast Bentgrass greens are what people talk about when they are finished with the round. These greens are probably some of the best greens that can be played in Myrtle

Beach. So take your time, keep your head steady, and watch the speed of the putt.

Wide fairways will accept the drive. So tee it high, and let it fly. However, the approach shots to the elevated greens have to be accurate; otherwise, the ball can land in a typical deep Winged Foot bunker. Unless bunker play is your forte, watch out.

SOUTH STRAND GOLF COURSES

South Strand golf courses are located within Surfside, Murrells Inlet, or Pawleys Island. If staying in accommodations in these areas, these courses are convenient with a minimum drive time.

TOURNAMENT PLAYERS CLUB OF MYRTLE BEACH
⭐ Must See!

(1199 TPC Blvd. 9, Murrells Inlet ☎ 843.357.3399

🖱 **tpc-mb.com)** The TPC of Myrtle Beach was designed by Tom Fazio and Lanny Wadkins. As with all the TPC courses around the country, when playing the TPC of Myrtle Beach, the golfer is playing a PGA-tour caliber golf course. The tees, fairways, bunkers, and greens are the same conditions that some of the greatest names in golf have played.

The course is carved out of the natural setting and surroundings of the Lowcountry of South Carolina. Expect to experience all that the Lowcountry nature has to offer here at the TPC, and that includes tall pines, marsh and wetlands, plus wildlife such as turkeys and eagles. Although located in the Lowcountry, don't expect to play a perfectly flat course. Fazio and Wadkins had plenty of earth moved to create some elevated tees and greens.

Golf

As with most of Fazio courses, accuracy is stressed whether off the tees or the approach shots. Many tee shots are forced carries, either over lakes or the Lowcountry wetlands. Not long ago the greens were resodded with MiniVerde Ultradwarf, which is the same grass that they play on at the famed Stadium Course at Sawgrass.

CALEDONIA GOLF AND FISH CLUB ✪ Must See!

(2200 Kings River Rd., Pawleys Island ☎ 843.237.3675 🖱 fishclub.com) Almost "perfect golf" is not too strong a phrase when describing Caledonia Golf and Fish Club designed by Mike Strantz. Although technically it was Strantz's first design, he was a former assistant of Tom Fazio, and he hit a "hole in one" here at Caledonia.

If first impressions are important, then plan to be impressed. Built on the site of a former rice plantation turned hunting and fishing retreat, the experience starts with the turn onto the drive up to the antebellum clubhouse. The 100-year old live oaks, dripping with Spanish moss, ooze Lowcountry and Old South charm.

Since it opened in 1994, Caledonia has been honored by all of the golf magazines. In 2009, Caledonia was named one of the best courses to play in the United States. Expect to play over wetlands and water on many holes. Don't expect houses and condos. The owners have stayed true to the natural setting of this course and kept it all natural. It's a must play for the dedicated golfer.

Golf

TRUE BLUE PLANTATION

(900 Blue Stem Dr., Pawleys Island ☎ 843.235.0900
🖱 truebluegolf.com) Just across from Caledonia Golf and
Fish Club on Kings River Road is its sister course, True Blue
Plantation. This course is very similar to Caledonia, just as
nice and just as beautiful. Also designed by Mike Strantz in
1998, True Blue has constantly been ranked as one of the best
courses in the United States.

True Blue was also built on a rice plantation, where they also
grew indigo, thus the name True Blue. It has wide fairways and
also some changes in elevation to challenge the golfer. Strantz
took a beautiful piece of property and put a beautiful golf
course that seems to enhance the surroundings.

WICKED STICK GOLF LINKS

(U.S. 17 Bypass, Surfside Beach ☎ 843.215.2500
🖱 wickedstick.com) John Daly collaborated with Clyde
Johnston in 1995 to design this course that seems to fit Daly's
personality perfectly. It is wide open with trouble scattered
about here and there. "Tee it high and let it fly" and "grip
it and rip it" will become part of the vocabulary during the
round at Wicked Stick.

This is a Links Style course that befits the 1995 winner of the
Open Championship. Golfers can expect to encounter deep
pot bunkers, dune-like mounds along with native grasses. Don't
look for any fairway bunkers however. Since this is South
Carolina, waterbodics and lakes are placed in strategic spots
along the course.

One thing that can be found on Wicked Stick and no other
course on the Grand Strand are the Daly tees. There are

Golf

selected holes that have these tees that Daly gives the golfer the "grip and rip it" chance. This is a fun addition and not extremely risky, since the landing area for all drives is generous.

John Daly also has a small museum on-site in the club house that is enjoyable with a fair amount of his mementos.

BLACKMOOR GOLF CLUB

(6100 Longwood Dr., Murrells Inlet ☎ 843.650.5555
🖱 Blackmoor.com) Blackmoor Golf Club was built in 1990 and is the first in South Carolina and the only course on the Grand Strand designed by former Open, Masters, and U.S. Open Champion Gary Player. Player's layout is on the site of a rice plantation. He did a great job with this course that sits close to, and in some instances parallels the Waccamaw River. As the course is being played, one cannot help but take in the beauty and characteristics of the South Carolina Lowcountry that include cypress, live oak trees, and tall pines.

Player made a very fair and playable course at Blackmoor. There is no trickery but a few of the dreaded blind shots that must be made, but with the ambience surrounding Blackmoor these can be forgiven. Expect to find plenty of water and wetlands at Blackmoor. It is not overly hard and is playable for all skill levels.

HERITAGE CLUB

(478 Heritage Dr., Pawleys Island ☎ 843.237.3424
🖱 legendsgolf.com/heritageclub) Another beautiful course in the Lowcountry and southern section of the Grand Strand is the Heritage Club. Designed by Dan Maples on 600 acres, it opened in 1986. It can be a challenge because of the narrow

Golf

fairways. The drive off the tee has to be well placed to ensure that the approach shot lands in a good spot on the undulating greens.

The challenge of the Heritage Club does not only include narrow fairways, but also plenty of water as do almost all the Lowcountry courses. Ten of the 18 holes on this course have water that can come into play. Although there is a generous portion of water on the front nine, water is more prevalent on the back nine, where an intimidating and big but beautiful lake will come into play around holes 12, 13, 14, and 18.

Fishing

The fishing laws in South Carolina changed in a significant way in 2009. Starting in July, everyone indulging in recreational fishing in the saltwater of South Carolina, whether it be from shore, bank, pier (public or private), must buy a recreational saltwater fishing license. This also pertains to those who are doing recreational crabbing or shrimping.

If the fisherman is under 16 years old, a license is not required. Other exemptions include those who are fishing off a licensed public pier or individuals fishing from a licensed fishing charter vessel. Also those who are crabbing are exempt if using three or fewer drop nets, or three or fewer traps.

The laws were enacted to provide better management of South Carolina's marine resources. The license can be purchased from almost any business that sells fishing equipment, whether it be a hardware or Super Wal-Mart. The license price for a South Carolina Resident is $10. For an annual non-resident's license, the price is $35. For non-residents who are only going to be in South Carolina for a short time, the state provides for a 14-day license that is $11.

Fish are expected to be running as follows: amberjack, barracuda, and blue fish, April through October; dolphin and flounder April through September; cobia June through October; red drum, king, and Spanish mackerel May through November; shark May through October; red fish and sea trout July through November; sea bass January through December; speckled trout and stripers January through March, November and December; spots October and November; tarpon January, February, and May through September.

Costs are fairly consistent from year to year. Notes suggest a comparison among listings ranging from least expensive ($) to average ($$) to most expensive ($$$).

FISHING PIERS

Myrtle Beach offers a wide array of choices for fishermen who prefer fishing off public piers rather than hiring charters.

APACHE PIER

(Lake Arrowhead Rd. ☎ 843.497.6486

🖱 apachefamilycampground.com) Located on the grounds at Apache Campground, fishermen will have to check in through the entrance gate at the campground to get access to the pier. However upon arrival, fishing can be done from what is billed as the longest pier on the east coast.

No South Carolina fishing license is required at the Apache Pier. The cost to fish from the pier is $8.50 for all day, for two rods. The pier is open from 6:00 a.m. until 11:00 p.m. every day of the week. The bait and tackle shop on-site has many different kinds of bait that will be needed to land the big one. Rods and reels can be rented for a daily fee. If crabbing is on the agenda, do not expect to rent nets, but you can purchase them at the tackle shop. The cost for crabbing off the pier is $6. If camping at the Apache Campground, a discount for fishing and crabbing is in effect. Just to walk out on the pier and enjoy the view is $1.

This is mainly a campground for families and not strictly a fishing pier, so expect lots of families. If a child is in the group and wants to fish, this may be the place to bring them simply because of the atmosphere that it possesses. *($)*

CHERRY GROVE FISHING PIER ✪ Must See!

(3500 N. Ocean Blvd., North Myrtle Beach ☎ 843.249.1625 🌐 cherrygrovepier.com) The Prince family knows the fishing pier business. This pier was built in the 1950s. The Prince family owned a nearby motel and bought the pier in the early 1960s. The 985-foot pier has been hit several times by hurricanes that either brushed the coast of South Carolina or made landfall somewhere along the coast of one of the Carolinas. Most damaging of those was Hugo that destroyed the pier, along with millions of dollars of other property in 1989. In 1999 Hurricane Floyd brushed by Cherry Grove and tore off the end of the pier and the two-story observation deck. That presented only a temporary problem for the Prince family. They got busy and rebuilt the end of the pier and had it ready for visitors and fishermen by the next spring.

This pier is known for more than getting hit by hurricanes. The pier is the site of a world record catch. In 1964, a 1780-pound tiger shark was caught off this pier. At the end of 2009, it was still the only all-tackle world record ever caught in South Carolina.

The bait and tackle shop at the pier has all that the fisherman must have for success. Rental gear and a fine line of name brand gear are offered. As far as bait is concerned, the staff can tell the fisherman what the fish are biting, whether it is mullet or bloodworms, night crawlers or sand fleas. It's all here.

The basic season is from February to December. The hours of operation are from 6:00 a.m. to midnight. However, during the winter, weather may permit only limited hours, so it's best to call to be sure of the hours of operation for a particular day.

Fishing **107**

No fishing license is needed to fish off Cherry Grove Pier. If a fisherman brings his own rod, the cost is $1.20 to get on the pier and $6 per rod that is used. Fishing for King Mackerel is $16 per day. Walkers can get on the pier for the $1.50 entrance fee.

Seeing the pier is a must, whether one fishes, photographs or simply appreciates the structure of the pier itself. *($)*

PIER 14

(1306 N. Ocean Blvd. ☎ 843.448.4314 🖱 pier14.com) Pier 14 is one tough pier. It is one of the only piers to survive Hurricane Hugo in 1989. It did have damage but was not a loss, as so much other property was after Hugo left its mark on the South Carolina coast. It took five months to get it back in shape and to welcome guests to the restaurant and fishermen to the pier.

All-day passes to fish are $6. Equipment rental is available for $12 with a $20 refundable deposit. Many kinds of bait are offered for more than 40 different kinds of fish that have been caught off this pier.

A very good restaurant is on-site with indoor and outdoor seating and a full bar, and many vacationers drop in for lunch or anglers come back at night after fishing on the pier all day. See the "Dining" chapter for details on the restaurant. *($)*

SECOND AVENUE PIER

(110 N. Ocean Blvd. ☎ 843.626.8480 🖱 secondavenuepier.com) The history of Second Avenue Pier goes back to the 1930s. All the piers along the coast, and especially those along the Grand Strand, have taken a pounding with the hurricanes. Second Avenue Pier is no exception. It was destroyed in 1954 by

Hurricane Hazel, and again in 1989 when Hugo came ashore at McClellanville, South Carolina. Between those disasters, it also took a major hit from Hurricane David in 1981.

Second Avenue Pier's season runs from Valentine's Day to Thanksgiving Day of each year. During the season it opens at 7:00 a.m. and usually closes at 11:00 p.m. depending on how busy they are and if the fish are biting. An all-day pass to fish on the pier is $8. This pass allows access to come and go as one pleases during business hours. Buying a fishing license is not required, as with all piers where payment is mandatory to fish, then the pier has paid all license fees. There is no limit as to how many fish can be caught.

The pier has a bait and tackle shop where both can be purchased. Rental rods are available for $9.65 a day and refundable deposit of $10. If a person would like to catch his or her own bait, nets and buckets are for sale. To take a stroll on the 906-foot pier costs $1.

Beer, wine, and liquor can be purchased at the restaurant, **Big Daddy's**, if needed. However fishermen can bring up to one six-pack along with them to the pier.

For all guests at the nearby **The Lighthouse Motel** fishing is free all day. On Wednesday nights during the summer people enjoy a free fireworks show at the pier. *($)*

SPRINGMAID PIER ✪ Must See!

(3200 Springmaid Blvd. ☎ 843.315.7156

⬤ springmaidbeach.com) Springmaid Pier is part of a 27-acre resort facility built by Col. E. W. Springs, the owner of cotton mills in Fort Mill in the Midlands area of South Carolina.

Very much committed to providing recreational facilities for his employees, Col. Springs built pools, accommodations, and bowling alleys for his employees in Fort Mill, Lancaster, and Kershaw, South Carolina. In 1949, he built a resort in Myrtle Beach for fun and recreation for his employees to come to the South Carolina coast.

The local newspaper each year has a "Best of the Beach" feature which tallies votes by the locals, and they have constantly named the Springmaid Pier the best pier along the Grand Strand. This popular fishing spot is more than 1,000 feet long and 36 feet wide accented with a 110-foot "T" at the very end.

There is very nice tackle shop at the pier. Rods can be rented for $9 a day, as is the cost of fishing all day on the pier. Bait can be bought for an extra $4.50. The fishing advice and tips are free and staff here is glad to hand it out anytime. Fishing is free for all guests who are staying at the resort. However, a fishing license is not required for anyone who fishes from the pier once the fishing pass has been purchased.

The pier is open for fishing from 6:00 a.m. until midnight each day. To walk on the pier is $1, and that fee is waived if staying at the resort. (*$*)

SURFSIDE PIER

(11 South Ocean Blvd., Surfside Beach ☎ 843.238.0121 🖱 surfsidepier.com) Surfside Pier was built in 1953. In the last 56 years, it has been rebuilt because of hurricane damage three times. **Pier Outfitters**, the bait and tackle shop located at the pier, rents rods for $9. In addition the fisherman must have a driver's license, and a deposit of $30 is required. A day pass for fishing on the pier costs $9. They also sell a weekly pass for $45. These passes allow the fisherman to have two rods or two crab nets, or one of each. King fishing is a little more expensive at $12.50 for the day and $65 for the weekly pass. This allows the fisherman to have the two bottom rods: one anchor rod and one fighting rod. To walk out on the pier is a small fee. No fishing license is required to fish on the pier. Also, beer or other alcohol can be brought on to the pier, or it can be purchased at Pier Outfitters. *($)*

THE PIER AT GARDEN CITY

(110 S. Waccamaw Dr., Garden City ☎ 843.651.9700

🖱 **pieratgardencity.com)** One thing that makes The Pier at Garden City unique among all the piers along the Grand Strand is that there is no charge to just go out and walk on the pier and see what the fishermen are catching or even if the fish are biting. One reason for this free walk could be a very nice bar at the end of the pier offering entertainment during the season.

The Pier at Garden City is open 24 hours a day during the season. There is a good tackle shop at the pier that rents rods for $9 plus a deposit of $15. They also have a varied array of bait and can tell the fisherman what the fish are hitting that particular day. The pier stretches out some 668 feet into the Atlantic Ocean. Although coolers filled with beer are not allowed, alcohol can be purchased at The Pier at Garden City.

To fish at the pier the charge is $9 for adults; children under 12 years can fish for half price. A weekly pass costs $45. No fishing license is required to fish at the pier. If someone does rent a rod at the tackle shop, when the pier is open 24 hours a day rods must be turned in at midnight. Also during this time the daily fishing pass expires at 6:00 a.m. *($)*

FISHING CHARTERS

Around the Myrtle Beach area, there are literally dozens and dozens of fishing charters and fishing boat captains. Those recommended are certainly not the only ones but are those that are known to have been here along the Grand Strand for a time that makes them well established. They know what and where to fish. Good judgment says that all potential customers of a fishing trip should ask the captain for references and to ask around for locals' recommendations prior to setting foot on the boat.

If planning an ocean fishing trip, know the difference between a charter boat and a party boat. A charter boat is usually licensed by the U.S. Coast Guard to carry only up to six fishermen. A reservation is needed, and usually a deposit is necessary. Charter boats are for the really serious anglers. Some charter boats are licensed to carry more than six fishermen and can be chartered for corporate outings or groups up to 75 people.

A party boat can carry many more fishermen and takes passengers on a first come first served basis. There is usually no need to make reservations unless calling for information and reserving space for a large number.

There are two distinctive types of fishing in the ocean: bottom and trolling. Bottom fishing is simply putting bait on the rig and dropping it in to find those fish that tend to stay close to the floor of the ocean. Grouper and snapper are the well-known ones. Most of the party boats are doing bottom fishing.

Trolling is mainly done on a charter, but not always. Trolling is when the bait on the line is barely below the surface of the water and is being pulled by a slow moving boat. The idea is to give the fish the impression that the bait is a slow moving fish that they may get for food. When the fisherman is trolling expectations are to catch, billfish, mackerel, and dolphin among others.

When the type of trip to take has been decided, then comes the question of what to take. A few things are mandatory. Always take some sunscreen and a cap or hat even if it is not sunny. Also, these boats are not in the food business, so take lunch or a snack and beverage, but no glass bottles. A jacket is probably a good idea, even in the summer. No need for ice, because that is provided. If the fish are going to be taken home, bring a cooler but leave it in the car as the boat has coolers. Last but not least, if someone has a propensity for seasickness, plan for that a few days before the trip by obtaining motion sickness pills or a patch that one can get from a doctor.

Regardless of which type of fishing trip is chosen, a captain and at least one mate will be on board. Although payment of the trip is made in advance, at the end of the trip which has been fun and fish have been caught, a tip for the crew is usually in order. This can be 15 to 20 percent depending on satisfaction and help that was given.

Price notes show comparisons among the listings, ranging from least expensive ($), average ($$) or most expensive ($$$).

CALABASH FISHING FLEET
(9945 Nance St., Calabash ☎ 910.575.0017
🖰 calabashfishingfleet.com) Calabash Fishing Fleet and Capt. Robert specialize mainly on party boat trips, but they can do

charter for groups up to 70 people. That half-day trip is $2,500 and the full-day trip is $3,500. Half-day fishing on the party boat is $40 for adults and $35 for children under 12. These trips leave in the morning and return at 12:30 p.m., and the afternoon half-day trip leaves at 2:00 p.m. and returns at 6:00 p.m. Capt. Robert has a Gulf Stream party boat with space to accommodate for easier fishing for $90 for adults and $80 for children. The captain wants no crowded boats and tangled lines, however, he does want plenty of fishing time. This trip leaves at 7:00 a.m. and returns at 6:00 p.m. Capt. Robert and crew provide the bait, tackle as well as ice for the catch upon return. Reservations are required, as is a 72-hour cancellation policy for all trips. *($$)*

CAPTAIN DICK'S

(4123 U.S. Bus 17, Murrells Inlet ☎ 843.651.3676
🖱 Captdicks.com) Captain Dick's has it all when it comes to fishing at Myrtle Beach, including large party boats and lots of charters. Captain Dick's is one of the most-recognized names in fishing around the Grand Strand. The company has experience to make the trip very enjoyable with everything needed for a successful excursion, such as rod, manual reel, bait, and tackle. Among the charters Captain Dick's offers a four-hour near shore and inlet trip for $425 and an off-shore eight-hour trolling trip for $875. These are perfect for the serious angler, in that they are reserved for only four. Party boat prices are $44 per adult for a four-and-a-half-hour trip, or $62 for an eight-hour trip that goes about 30 miles off shore. An all-day, 12-hour Gulf Stream trip is $90. Discounts are offered for children on all of these trips. About once a month or when Capt. Dick gets enough real anglers, an overnight Gulf Stream trip is

planned. This trip leaves at 1:30 p.m. on Saturday and returns 2:30 p.m. on Sunday. Cost for this trip is $175 per fisherman. An electric reel can be rented on these trips for $12.50. *($$)*

CAPTAIN SMILEY'S FISHING CHARTERS

(Waterfront, Little River ☎ 843.361.7445
⬤ captainsmileyfishingcharters.com) Capt. Patrick Kelly, better known as Capt. Smiley gives the angler that personal touch on his fishing charter trips. One to three fishermen is what he usually takes out, so expect no crowding or getting lines tangled on his excursions. He has spent his whole life on the water and wants his clients to experience the same exuberance that he has each time he goes out on a trip. Capt. Smiley provides all tackle and bait needed. Just bring the essentials that are needed for a half or full day of fishing: some food and snacks, sunscreen and enthusiasm for fishing. *($$)*

CATCH-1 CHARTERS

(Murrells Inlet ☎ 843.450.1330 ⬤ catch-1familyfun.com) Capt. Shannon Currie has been fishing the waters around Myrtle Beach and Murrells Inlet since the 1980s. Catch-1 Charters is a family-oriented fishing charter offering only inshore trips around the estuaries and inlet creeks of Murrells Inlet. They welcome fishermen of all ages. When fishing the inshore waters, there is little or no seasickness because of calmer waters than the ocean. There are half-day charters for one fisherman at $250, $325 for two, and for three or four, the cost is $425. An additional $75 per person is charged if there are more than four people. Cruises are available at $75 per hour for up to six people. *($$)*

EXTREME FISHERMAN CHARTERS

(Murrells Inlet ☎ 843.344.0974 🖱 extremefisherman.com)

Extreme Fisherman Charters is a family run charter with Capt. Pete Mercuro and his son Capt. Jeff. Through his corporate business days, Capt. Pete has fished all over the southern part of the country. His Atlantic Ocean fishing inevitably led him to Myrtle Beach where he opened this company in 2002. Extreme Fisherman Charters offers inshore and near shore charters. This provides the advantage of fishing calmer waters, the opportunity for more fishing time since there are no long boat rides to get 15 to 20 miles off shore and the use of light tackle. When fishing inshore and near shore, the angler is not governed by the weather as much as when the ocean gets too choppy to go out. One can expect to catch spots, flounder, and trout. Near shore expect to catch mackerel, cobia, and pompano. A half-day charter (four hours) for one or two fishermen is offered for $375 and a shorter three-hour trip for $275. For more than two there is an additional charge of $50 per fisherman. On occasion a full day charter is available. *($$)*

FISHER OF MEN CHARTERS

(3370 Hwy. 50, Little River ☎ 843.249.8662

🖱 **fisherofmencharter.com)** Randy Elliot has more than 30 years of fishing experience around Little River Neck and the ocean out from North Myrtle Beach. Capt. Randy does not do party boat trips, but strictly fishing charter trips. He does allow more than six fishermen on board at an extra charge of $40 to $70. Capt. Randy has a $500 half-day fishing charter for six. A six-hour trip is $650, and an eight-hour trip runs $900. On these trips, one can expect to fish for king mackerel, Spanish mackerel, sea bass, and shark. The Gulf Stream trip, which is a 12 hour trip, costs $1,400 with a $100 fee for additional fishermen. These trips are fishing for dolphin, bass, barracuda, and maybe some grouper. *($$)*

GO FISH

(2201 Little River Neck Rd., North Myrtle Beach ☎ 843.333.3920
💧 fishnorthmyrtlebeach.com) Although Capt. Chris Gill has done a lot of deep-sea fishing and led many deep-sea fishing trips, he does not offer those type fishing charters now. He loves his fishing inshore. His charters go to the estuaries, rivers, and bays of near shore ocean waters to catch reds, flounder, Spanish mackerel, and blues to name a few species. Families and children are welcome on the Go Fish and inshore fishing charters. Capt. Chris offers a half-day for up to three people for $220, with a charge of $40 for an additional person. The whole-day charter is $440 for up to three anglers. One more person can be added for $60. All bait and fishing tackle are included in these prices. *($$)*

HURRICANE FLEET

(9975 Nance St., Calabash ☎ 910.579.3660
💧 hurricanefleet.com) The Hurricane Fleet is one of the oldest fishing fleets in the area with more than 25 years of experience fishing the waters of both North Carolina and South Carolina. The company has four boats, the longest being 90 feet and the smaller at 40 feet. The regular trips include both trolling and bottom fishing. The ultimate fishing trip is the 12- to 16-hour excursion to the Gulf Stream to catch tuna, wahoo, and the occasional marlin. Prices start at $40 for half-day trips that leave twice a day at 8:00 a.m. and again at 1:00 p.m. Gulf Stream trips are $85. Both of these price points are for the

party boat. Charter boat trips for up to six people are $550 for half-day trips that leave twice a day: 7:00 a.m. and 1:00 p.m. Full-day trips for up to six people are $950. To get to the Gulf Stream for up to six people is $1,500. The overnight Gulf Stream Trip leaves at 6:00 p.m. returning to Calabash at 10:00 a.m. and is $75. *($$)*

LITTLE RIVER FISHING FLEET

(BW's Marina, Little River ☎ 843.361.3323 ▮ littleriverfleet.com) This company has about 17 years of experience. It is accessible from Mineola Avenue which is easy to find in Little River. Two boats offer cruises for half a day, three quarters of a day, Gulf Stream, or shark fishing. All of these trips are offered as trolling or bottom fishing. They also go out as far as 60 miles for tuna fishing. *($$)*

MARLIN QUAY MARINA

(1508 Waccamaw Dr., Murrells Inlet ☎ 843.651.4444 ▮ marlinquay.net) Marlin Quay Marina specializes in charter fishing in the waters in Myrtle Beach. That can mean the creeks and inlets around Murrells Inlet and Pawley's Island to the Gulf Stream. Depending on which boat the group decides to charter, prices for a half-day run from $375 to $775. Three-quarter day-fishing charters cost from $600 to $1,100. Full day trips are from $775 to $1,400. Gulf Stream charters are from $1,295 to $2,200. Regardless of the trip taken, the boat leaves the dock at 7:00 a.m., except the Gulf Stream trip which leaves at 5:00 a.m. A half-day shark-fishing trip is also available. Included on all trips are all bait and tackle, ice, and fish cleaning – and of course a certified USCG Captain and a mate. *($$)*

SOUTHERN EXPOSURE CHARTERS

(4031 U.S. 17 Bus., Murrells Inlet ☎ 843.241.2376
🖱 **dogsfish2.com)** Capt. Tom Beckham and Southern Exposure
Charters does not have party boats for large groups of fishermen. It also has no walkups to jump on board for a day of
fishing. Capt. Beckham only takes four fishermen at a time
for his charter. His main two objectives on a charter are safety
and that everyone has a good time. Capt. Tom is serious about
fishing. However, he does offer a variety of charters for the
novice who just wants to experience ocean fishing such as a
half-day charter for $550.

Southern Exposure offers the 12-hour Gulf Stream trip for
$1,250. On this trip the boat is trolling and drifting 45 to 60
miles off shore for tuna, wahoo, dolphin, and bill fish. On the
full day trip ($950), anglers spend ten hours on the water. This
includes both trolling and bottom fishing for grouper, trigger,
and sea bass. All of these trips leave approximately at first light
of day.

Fishermen can also take shark home, provided that the fish
caught is of legal size and not protected by law. However, don't
expect to keep them if you are not going to eat your catch. If
planning to keep some, be sure to have a cooler handy when
arriving ashore. *($$)*

THE NEW DOUBLE R FISHING CHARTER SERVICE

(Little River ☎ 843.249.1889 🖱 newdoubler.com) Capt. Ricky
Long was born in Little River and has been fishing the area all
his life. His father started doing charters more than 60 years
ago. Ricky knows some of the best fishing spots along the
waterway and ocean. He says "you come back to the dock with

a smile," so he must know something. He tries to make the fishing experience enjoyable and to make your trip worth the money. Capt. Ricky has two half-day charters, one that leaves in the morning and the other at 1:00 p.m. priced at $600 for up to six fishermen. A three-quarter day charter that goes about 20 miles is priced at $1,000 for up to six anglers. The 12-hour Gulf Stream charter is $1,500 for six fishermen. Capt. Ricky can also customize party boats or have a night cruise for $100 per hour with a three-hour minimum. *($$)*

VOYAGER FISHING FLEET

(9931 Nance St., Calabash ☎ 843.626.9500

🖱 voyagerfishingcharters.com) Voyager Fishing Fleet specializes in blue-water trolling and also has Gulf Stream bottom fishing. A trolling or bottom-fishing trip leaves at 7:30 a.m. and returns at noon, traveling approximately 15 miles off shore with rates starting at $425. This company also offers an eight-hour Gulf Stream special that travels almost 30 miles off shore for up to six people costing $750. This leaves at 7:30 a.m. and returns at 3:00 p.m. Discounts are available for multiple day charters. *($$)*

Water Sports

A beach vacation is left incomplete if vacationers don't indulge in and take advantage of water sports that the area offers. Of course water sports and all that goes along with them, are at a premium all up and down the Grand Strand. Whether the visitors are looking for water parks, fishing trips, parasailing, or Jet Ski riding, they will not have to look very far. There are plenty of choices, whether vacationing in the north, central, or the southern section of the Grand Strand.

The parasailing and banana boat rides are seasonal in Myrtle Beach. For the most part, the season runs from Easter to Labor Day. These times may be extended or shortened depending on the weather conditions. For instance, if Easter happens to fall in March, it may be too cold for these activities.

BOB'S WATER SPORTS

(2208 N. Ocean Blvd., North Myrtle Beach ☎ 843.249.9908 ☗ bobswatersports.com) Bob's Water Sports is located in the Cherry Grove section of North Myrtle Beach, a beautiful part of the Grand Strand. It is open for parasailing and banana boat rides during the season. The parasail can take three people or up to a maximum of 450 pounds. There is a price advantage to going with two friends. Bob's ferries the customer out to the parasailing boat via the Red Dog Banana Boat. Vacationers can also ride the Red Dog Banana Boat for a 15-minute ride along the Cherry Grove coast. *($)*

CAPT. DICK'S

(Waterfront, Murrells Inlet ☎ 843.491.4324 🌐 captdicks.com)

Although most locals think of Capt. Dick's for fishing, many other water sports are also offered. Parasailing is one of the most popular activities. The boat departs from the dock at Capt. Dick's at the waterfront in Murrells Inlet. Once out in the ocean, customers are launched from the deck of the captain's boat for close to a one-hour ride above the Atlantic at a cost of $55. Customers younger than 18 years must have an adult present and those over 18 must have picture identification. Reservations are not required but are suggested.

The Jet Ski and wave runner rentals are $79 for a one-hour ride through inlet channels and the ocean, if the ocean conditions are favorable. Up to three people can get on one of the wave runners. The person who signs the rental contract must be over 18 years old, and drivers must be at least 16 years old. As with the parasailing, there is no minimum age to ride along but the rider must be large enough to fit into one of the life jackets provided. Instructions on safety are given before the ride can begin. Reservations are not required but are urged.

Capt. Dick's also rents boats for fishing or just for sightseeing. These boats hold up to five people not to exceed 1,000 pounds. Also available are pontoon boats that are great for sightseeing through the inlet or for fishing. These boats hold up to ten people. Kayak rental is also very popular if the vacationer wants to provide his or her own power throughout the marsh and inlet. Rates for boats run from $269 for all day on the pontoon to $25 for four hours with the kayak. There is no refund for returning boats early.

To view nature in the inlet, Capt. Dick's offers the dolphin watch aboard the Sea Thunder. This trip carries the nature lover through the channels and marshes of Murrells Inlet to view the beautiful scenery, birds and other wildlife, then to the ocean and to Surfside Beach where dolphins can be seen frequently. *($$)*

DOWNWIND WATER SPORTS
(2915 Ocean Blvd. ☎ 843.448.7245

⛟ downwindsailsmyrtlebeach.com) Downwind Water Sports is located oceanfront in Myrtle Beach beside **Damon's Oceanfront** which is a restaurant with a great view albeit not always the best food or service. Downwind also has a location at 5th Ave. N in Surfside Beach known as **Shoreline Water Sports**. Both locations together offer almost any water sport that one would want while at the beach, from parasailing, banana boat rides, and Jet Ski riding, to ocean kayaks and catamaran tours. In addition, kite boarding with lessons is also a sport for the more adventurous vacationer. They definitely know what they are doing because they have been in business since 1981, and that makes them the oldest water sports company along the Grand Strand.

Jet skis are either single or tandem and come with instructions for first timers. The banana boat rides are a wet experience, so make sure the bathing suit is on. It is a great way to beat the heat when that South Carolina sun is beating down. Riding the waves in a kayak is another way to cool off. If you see people kayaking in the ocean riding the waves or just cruising along the coast, it's apparent that this is great fun. The sail boat rental is fantastic. The renter may need to take the 30-minute lesson first, which is $65, but with that comes a 30-minute sail time.

However, if someone is not completely comfortable going alone, they may be in the mood for the catamaran tour. This includes a trip from Myrtle Beach to Surfside. The cat is large enough for up to six people with everything provided for a safe trip. *($$)*

EXPRESS WATER SPORTS

(U.S. 17 Bus., Murrells Inlet ☎ 843.357.7777

🖰 **expresswatersports.com)** Express Water Sports offers parasailing, banana boats and kayak rentals, as well as a dolphin cruise or a sunset cruise. The folks at Express Water Sports emphasize safety for all of their customers, especially for those who chose to parasail. They do not discriminate against anyone since they consider this a sport for all ages and also for those that are physically challenged. If you do choose to parasail with Express Water Sports, expect to fly some 500 feet above the Atlantic Ocean at full height. The parasailing boat can carry up to 12 people, so if there is a full load of 12, expect to be out on the water for about two hours.

If the choice is to rent a kayak, expect to have a guided naturalist tour through the creeks, marshes, and channels of Murrells Inlet. Single and double kayaks are available, the prices for which begin at $30. Bug repellent is often needed, as well as clothes and shoes that will not get damaged if they get wet. Self-guided tours are also available, with prices starting at $15.

The banana boat ride begins at the dock in Murrells Inlet and proceeds to the wide open Atlantic. It is billed as the longest ride of the beach. The cost for this is $25. *($)*

MYRTLE BEACH WATER SPORTS

(Waterfront, Little River; 17th Ave. S., North Myrtle Beach; Waterway at Holiday Inn West, Myrtle Beach Socastee; Murrells Inlet ☎ 843.497.8848/843.361.3322 ☏ myrtlebeachwatersports.com) Myrtle Beach Water Sports is the buffet of water activities in the Myrtle Beach area. Rentals include jet skis, pontoon boats, and jet boats, plus parasailing, dolphin cruises, and Jet Ski dolphin-watch tours. Unfortunately Myrtle Beach Water Sports does not offer all of these at every location. However, with access to an automobile, the vacationer can get to a location for the desired activity.

Jet Skis are rented at Little River, both of the Myrtle Beach locations (Socastee and on the waterway at the Holiday Inn West) and Murrells Inlet. All of these are on the Intracoastal Waterway and the renter may have up to 20 miles to ride. The Holiday Inn West location has the added feature of connection to the Waccamaw River which has beautiful sites, which affords glimpses of some wonderful wildlife.

Jet-ski drivers must be 16 years old and have photo identification. Any age can ride along with an adult driver. There is a 30-minute minimum. Apart from the Intracoastal, the Little River location offers the opportunity to get to the ocean for riding. This is also the location that offers the Sea Screamer speed boat that gives vacationers the two-hour dolphin cruise.

The North Myrtle beach location is at 17th Ave. S. This is an oceanfront location that offers parasailing and banana boat rides.

The Myrtle Beach locations in Socastee and at the Holiday Inn West also offer jet boat rentals on the Intracoastal Waterway. The nine-passenger jet boat gives riders the chance to view nature and possibly do some tubing on the Intracoastal over a journey of 20 miles. Riders are allowed to bring coolers and snacks if they choose to.

The Little River and both Myrtle Beach locations have pontoon boat rentals, a great way to take an unhurried trip up and down the Intracoastal. This is perfect for small groups to cruise and picnic and fish if they choose. The fishermen must get their own South Carolina licenses. There are small islands that can be perfect for a lunch or just some private time. *($$)*

MYRTLE WAVES WATER PARK
(U.S. 17 Bypass & 10 Ave. N. ☎ 843.918.8725
🖱 myrtlewaves.com) Myrtle Waves Water Park is the largest water park in South Carolina with attractions spread over 20 acres. All of the rides and slides contain over one million gallons of water. It is also one of the most popular water parks in South Carolina attracting over 200,000 visitors a year.

The park has eight water slides. The most exciting could be the Turbo Twister that starts out ten stories high and includes three enclosed dark tubes sending the rider toward the water level below at 50 feet per second. Halfway up the Turbo Twist are the Riptides Rockets. These are side-by-side slides that are 350 feet long, sending the rider airborne just before splashing down.

Snake Mountain features three serpentine inner tube slides: The Python, Water Moccasin, and The King Cobra. The Python is meant for parents taking small children down the slide. The Water Moccasin is fun for the whole family. The King Cobra is meant for the most adventurous and not suitable for small children.

Other slides include the Thunder Bolt, which is a toned down version of the Riptides Rockets. The Sidewinder is aimed for children that are less than 48 inches tall and cannot take advantage of the other slides.

Myrtle Waves also has two raft rides. The LayZee River speeds along at three miles per hour and all ages can participate. The Racin' River goes slightly faster at ten miles per hour.

Lifeguards are on duty at all times. There is some seating for resting when not sliding or on the raft rides. Covered cabanas can be rented to get out of the sun. There are also shaded pavilions for large groups. Visitors can make use of the showers, changing areas, and lockers.
Group rates are available. *($$)*

WILD WATER & WHEELS
(910 U.S. 17 S., Surfside Beach ☎ 843.238.3787
☏ wild-water.com) Wild Water & Wheels bills itself as "more than a water park." On the 16-acre facility, customers find a water park with a miniature golf putting course and a go-cart racing course called the Racezone. On the water park section, there are some 24 water slides. These include the Free Fall Cliff Dive, The Triple Dip, The Serpentine, and the Side Winder. Sliders must be at least 48 inches tall to participate on the Free Fall Cliff slide and the Triple Dip. If they do measure up, they can reach speeds up to 45 miles per hour, through a tunnel that opens up to an almost vertical drop. Forty-two inches is the requirement for the Serpentine and Side Winder. All of these slides are body-only slides. However, mats are provided for the Twin Twister, Head Rush, and Wild h2o Racer. All participants must be at least 42 inches tall for these slides.

Just as the mats are provided for the slides, tubes are provided for the Tube Slides and other attractions. These include the Wipe Out Wave Pool that sports some waves four feet high. The Dark Hole got the vote from *Southern Living* magazine as the number one scary ride in Myrtle Beach. The scary part is the entry of an almost-enclosed slide. Riders can use one or two tubes on the White Water Express as it twists and turns. Finally, a tube is the best way to float the 950-foot Lazy River that has waterfalls and raindrop fountains for the floaters. Bumper boats always create a big splash with visitors who love to bump and jostle other boaters.

Lockers and showers are for changing if desired. There is also a snack bar. Vending machines are placed throughout the park. The charge to get in the park in 2009 ranged from $18.40 to $29.25, beginning with the rate for children under 48 inches tall and for senior citizens. Children under two years old are free. Afternoon specials begin at 2:00 p.m. However, do not go to the park and expect to do the water slides, lazy river, and other pools. If visitors want to take advantage of the miniature golf course and the go carts, a $10 fee is added to the price. *($$)*

Gambling

Thousands upon thousands of people from all over the world come to the Myrtle Beach area every year, whether it is for the sun, the ocean, or the golf. However, there is a slowly swelling number of visitors who head to Myrtle Beach for a completely different reason. They come to the Grand Strand for the roulette, slot machines, Texas hold'em, and other games of chance.

Yes, one can come to the Grand Strand and gamble. It is not, however, the glitz, neon, and the strip of Las Vegas. Although there is plenty of neon in Myrtle Beach and U.S. 17 is called by some visitors "The Strip," it is a far cry from the gambling oasis in the desert of the western United States. So don't come to Myrtle Beach and expect to see lines and lines of casinos. In fact, unless someone knows where to go to participate in gaming on the Grand Strand, they may even miss it entirely! However, it can be said that one cannot legally gamble in South Carolina; so technically there is no gambling in Myrtle Beach. Technicalities aside, though, people do come to the area to gamble.

How? You may well ask. What visitors do is they travel to the northern part of Horry County to the small fishing village of Little River and board a boat that takes them on a 30-minute trip out in the ocean. Then and only then, do the games of chance begin, and everyone is welcome to "let it ride."

Why the 30-minute ride in the ocean? It takes approximately that long for the boat to get to what the United States Government considers International Waters. International Waters is an area beginning three miles off the coast of every country. They arrived at this magical number defining three miles as

International Waters in the 18th century, when a cannon shot from the coastline would travel approximately three miles. Thus, this was the distance that a country could defend its boarders from attack; space within that three-nautical mile distance was considered a part of the country.

Once out in International Waters, the boats are not governed by the state of South Carolina and can get down to business, which is gambling. The boats cruise around for about five hours on "a cruise to nowhere." On board are people who must be at least 21 years old with proof of age required, hoping to hit it big before they get back to Little River.

These boats have been steeped in controversy with the state of South Carolina in general and Little River and the county in particular. However the casino boats have managed to survive in spite of both the state legislature and the local governments. After more than ten years of existence, the boats have now become almost like neighbors.

SUN CRUZ CASINO

(4495 Mineola Ave., Little River ☎ 843.280.2933
⬤ suncruzcasino.com) Sun Cruz has been in Little River taking gamblers out on cruises almost from the beginning of gambling boats in South Carolina. They have a shuttle bus that picks gamblers up at various spots along the Grand Strand. At times this shuttle goes as far as Surfside Beach to pick up customers; however, it should be noted that the shuttle may not be going that far south every day of the year, so one would be advised to check with the office for information on the shuttle. Reservations are advised on the shuttle bus as well as each cruise. There is free parking if gamblers choose to drive to the dock.

There are no scheduled trips on Monday at Sun Cruz. However, Tuesday through Sunday there is a morning and evening cruise. From Tuesday to Thursday, the morning cruise leaves at 11:00 a.m. and returns at 4:15 p.m. Saturday and Sunday cruises leave at noon and return at 5:15 p.m. Evening cruises depart at 7:00 p.m. and return at 12:15 a.m. on Sundays through Thursdays, and 1:00 a.m. on Friday and Saturdays.

Sun Cruz has many slots on board for enjoyment. Some of the slots are the 5-cent variety and others range up to $25. Table bets are a $2 minimum, up to $500. The ever popular roulette and dice games are some of the favorite table games that can be found on board. An added feature is sports betting.

THE BIG "M" CASINO

(4491 Mineola Ave., Little River ☎ 843.249.9811 bigmcasino.com) There are no cruises on Mondays, but on other days, there are two cruises: morning and evening. On Saturday and Sunday a cruise leaves at 11:45 a.m. and returns at 5:00 p.m. From Tuesday to Friday, the first cruise leaves at 10:45 a.m. and returns at 4:00 p.m. On each Sunday, Tuesday, Wednesday, and Thursday a cruise leaves at 6:45 p.m. and returns at 11:45 p.m. Friday and Saturday evening cruises leave at 6:45 p.m. and return at midnight. The cost of each cruise is $10.

Big "M" Casino offers Black Jack tables with $10 minimum and $500 maximum; $25 minimum to $1,000 maximum; $50 minimum to $1,000 maximum. Also offered are roulette and three-card poker with a $5 minimum. There are many slots for those who do not want to get involved with the card games. Dice games are not on all cruises, so check with information at the office to determine when it is offered.

Most of the cruises at Big "M" offer a buffet for enjoyment, but it is not required that it be purchased. Alcoholic beverages cannot be taken on board, but they are sold on the boat. To board the boat a photo identification is required that proves age of 21 or above. Reservations are recommended, but are only held until 30 minutes before the boat departs. Special offers are advertised in local newspapers. There is free parking at the dock and office at Big "M."

Gambling

Dining

The Myrtle Beach area boasts more than 1,500 places to eat. This includes many which are locally owned and one-of-a-kind, with a few fine dining establishments and dozens of good casual restaurants. Fast food or franchise choices can be found on almost any corner, and the visitor will have no problem finding familiar names. The suggested dining options are the businesses with established reputations which are not likely to be here today and gone tomorrow.

To enjoy the best taste that a destination offers, visitors should dine at local restaurants. After all, who wants to go on vacation and eat the same foods that remind one of home? However, some guests, especially those visiting from overseas or rural areas may prefer a recognizable chain to avoid an adventurous experience. If so, these are a few suggestions of the tried and true family-friendly stops which offer table service from among a long list available: **TGI Friday's, Bone Fish, Red Lobster, Olive Garden, Damon's Grill, Sticky Fingers, Tony Roma's, Chili's, Bob Evans,** and **Cracker Barrel**.

Dining with a water view or other spectacular view is also a good idea to take full advantage of the visit to a beautiful destination. A few of the best restaurants, unfortunately, have no view, but there are many good ones on the oceanfront, at marinas overlooking creeks or along the Intracoastal Waterway, plus a few on lakes or golf courses.

While plenty of restaurants are available, the thousands of visitors converging on all of them at dinner time during the high season can create a challenging experience. It's common to wait an hour, or maybe two hours, for some of the favorite spots, especially during June and July. Some accept reservations, but many do not. Early-bird offers are prevalent and would be advisable for the elderly or families with small children who are on mealtime schedules. If specific choices are important, it's a good idea to call ahead and ask about reservations or whether a wait should be expected. Then it may be possible to get on a seating list before starvation sets in. Nevertheless, be prepared to browse through neighboring shops or chat at the bar while waiting to be seated. All of these suggested here are family-friendly as is most dining in the Myrtle Beach area, although the more upscale ones as noted would not be suitable for small children. Tipping of 15 percent to 20 percent is expected at full-service restaurants. Table or beverage service at buffet restaurants may warrant tipping at a smaller percentage, but it is not required for limited service.

The best experience sometimes can be found with the chef's specials where daily or seasonal creations reflect the freshest local ingredients as well as the culinary training. These specials are not always the best prices, although they may be choice items which are not regularly on the menu.

SEAFOOD

Seafood is either a specialty or offered in the entrées in almost every restaurant due to the coastal location which offers a bountiful catch fresh from the ocean, the rivers, or the creeks any time of year. Although a restaurant may specialize in seafood, a few vegetarian or meat entrées will usually be offered too.

Fish is caught locally year-round, especially in Murrells Inlet which proclaims itself "The Seafood Capital of the World" and in Calabash, North Carolina, which is the "Seafood Capital of North Carolina." Cobia, tarpon, and shark are caught in the Atlantic waters during the summer, and red snapper also is found off shore, while redfish and flounder are fished year-round. King mackerel, black bass, and grouper are available during specific seasons too.

She Crab Soup is made from the roe of the female crab and when homemade can be a sought-after specialty of a few restaurants. It's a creamy concoction often lightly flavored with a swirl of brandy which is sometimes optional.

Oysters are served in many restaurants year-round, although the season for harvesting locally is from September through April. During the winter months, a big pot of roasted oysters may be found at true local restaurants. The steam pot is a combination of oysters with other shellfish such as clams or shrimp and sometimes crab legs. Sometimes, it also includes corn-on-the-cob and is seasoned with spicy flavoring. If the month has an "R" in it, the oysters will be the freshest. Although this originated many years ago when refrigeration had not been invented for nationwide shipping, it remains a true measure, as the cooler coastal waters generate the largest and tastiest mollusk. See the "Events" chapter for suggested festivals featuring oysters, a great time to sample different preparations without ordering an entrée.

Shrimp is an important product which keeps many local fishermen in business. It began as a major South Carolina industry in the 1920s and growing significantly in the 1950s. The locally harvested shrimp are wild caught shrimp, which means that they are not baited but are caught in offshore waters in trawl nets pulled behind a boat. They are iced or placed in brine-freezing tanks on the boat and supplied as fresh frozen all year. The season begins in May or June for white shrimp; brown shrimp is available in June through fall; the largest product is the white shrimp caught annually in August, September, and October. Local restaurants often advertise if they are using local shrimp and sometimes display the seal denoting the logo for Wild American Shrimp. Although personal preference may dictate a liking for large imported shrimp, the freshest local product is definitely recommended for its distinctive taste.

Crab legs are not locally harvested from the coast along South Carolina, yet most seafood buffets and occasionally other menus do offer crab legs. They will be prepared from frozen Alaskan king crab and are a popular item with many seafood lovers on any visit to the coast.

Calabash is a term frequently used to refer to any lightly breaded and fried seafood. Calabash is a small fishing community in the southern corner of North Carolina, immediately bordering South Carolina. Two families began cooking seafood there in the 1930s. Today the cooking style can be found anywhere in the area, and is not very distinguishable from fried seafood anywhere else. Jimmy Durante and his wife frequently dined in **Coleman's**, one of those original establishments. The remembered closing of many of his shows was said to be a private message to his wife: Good night, Mrs. Calabash, wherever you are. See the "Dining" chapter for recommended restaurants located in Calabash.

CHICKEN BOG

Many cooks throughout South Carolina claim their own secret recipe for this dish, and few will share the details without leaving out a tiny ingredient which can make all the difference in the taste. In general it's a big pot of rice and chicken with some very fat broth and various spices. It sometimes includes chopped vegetables such as onion, celery, or green pepper. Smoked sausage is also used often. Bacon or butter is possibly added to be sure to create an extremely rich and juicy dish. It's not likely that anything instant is used either. Patience is required for the cooking process with little or no stirring allowed. The chicken bog is celebrated in a week long festival: the **Loris Bog-Off**. See the "Events" chapter for details of this 30-year-old tradition centered around a cooking competition.

LOCAL PRODUCE

Locally grown vegetables and fruits also are recommended, as they will often be picked on the farms of the neighboring rural areas and shipped into restaurants for daily serving. Growing seasons also dictate the best for each time period. Strawberries arrive in April; tomatoes, squash, cucumbers, and watermelon peak in June; peaches are ripe in August; corn is plentiful in September; apples are especially good in October. Root vegetables such as sweet potatoes and beets are plentiful in October and November. Winter vegetables grown locally are the hearty leafy greens such as collards and kale.

Farmers' markets are great shopping venues for condo renters or long-term visitors who choose to cook their own meals. Markets are usually outdoors and are open seasonally from summer through fall.

Sweet Tea is a traditional iced tea throughout many southern states. It's likely to be served when tea is ordered, unless the specific request is for unsweetened tea or hot tea. Yes, this is truly a southern thing. The secret to sweet tea being delicious is that it's sugared (with real sugar, nothing artificial) while hot. Half and half refers to half sweet and half unsweetened.

Dining is an important part of a vacation and has the power to create a memorable experience of the holiday destination for visitors. In addition to a few special recommendations, the restaurants are presented alphabetically within their general location on the Grand Strand. While it is not uncommon to travel from one end of the beach to another for a meal, it is usually preferable to enjoy the good choices within a close range from lodging.

Prices are shown for comparison purposes rather than with specific costs as Least Expensive $; Average $$; Most Expensive $$$.

CENTRAL MYRTLE BEACH RESTAURANTS

Central Myrtle Beach includes the area within the city limits of Myrtle Beach. This section offers convenient dining choices with a minimum of driving time if accommodations are within the central area.

ABUELO'S

(740 Coastal Grande Cir. ☎ 843.448.5533 🖳 abuelos.com) It's probably the numero uno choice for Mexican food. Although it is a chain located in about 15 states, this is the only one in South Carolina. Traditional enchiladas, tacos, and fajitas plus house specialties and combination plates offer many varieties of chicken, seafood, beef, and award-winning desserts. The steaming hot food is tasty and always served promptly. Menus for senior citizens and children are also extensive. *($)*

BUMMZ

(2002 N. Ocean Blvd. ☎ 843.916.9111 🖱 bummz.com) Walking in from the beach is acceptable for this casual spot which has outdoor and indoor seating. Located directly on the oceanfront in an original beach home in the middle of Myrtle Beach, this restaurant offers one of the best views in the area. The menu of wraps, salads, and sandwiches is especially pleasing for lunch. *($)*

CAPTAIN GEORGE'S

(1401 29th Ave. N. ☎ 843.916.2278 🖱 captaingeorges.com) When a huge seafood buffet is wanted, this is one of the best. Some 70 items are included along with meats, vegetables, and outstanding desserts. The focus is seafood, including raw, steamed, baked, and fried entrées, but plenty of meats, poultry, salads, and hot vegetable dishes are available too. It's open for dinner year-round except on Christmas Day and lunch at noon on Sundays. A few Virginia cities and one North Carolina city claim one of this chain, but there are no others in South Carolina. The regular price is $28.99 for adults; children between the ages of five and 12 are half price; younger children are free with beverage purchase. *($$)*

CAROLINA ROADHOUSE

(4617 N. Kings. Hwy. at 47th Ave. ☎ 843.497.9911 🖱 carolinaroadhouse.com) Casual business lunches are happening daily at tables next to visitors with the open kitchen

out fresh foods in a spacious, open dining room and
.. Two **Carolina Dreaming** restaurants are considered
cousins with the same menu, although different décor. The
big salads are among the favorites, with choices of salmon or
chicken toppings. The honey-drizzled croissant is included as a
special treat. Lunch and dinner are served daily. *($)*

CHEESEBURGER IN PARADISE

(850 N. Kings. Hwy. ☎ 843.448.9293
☻ cheeseburgerinparadise.com) Choose a tropical drink sporting
an umbrella, listen to live or recorded music direct from
Margaritaville (well, almost), and dine on large entrées of
sliders or burgers. The sweet potato fries and black bean soup
are especially good choices for sides or appetizers. Traditional
American fare with Caribbean flavor appeals to every age. It's
a casual and fun atmosphere. This themed chain restaurant is
located in about 15 states, but no others are in South Carolina.
Lunch and dinner are served daily. *($$)*

COLLECTOR'S CAFÉ

(7740 Kings Hwy. ☎ 843.449.9370
☻ collectorscafeandgallery.com) It's much more than a restau-
rant. It's an art gallery exhibiting fine local product from 40
artists including the owners Michael Craig and Thomas Davis.
In fact, everything throughout several rooms is for sale. Dinner
is served daily except Sunday, but it's a nice spot for browsing
art during the afternoon. The Mediterranean menu changes
seasonally with creative seafood and veal presentations and a
good wine list. The upscale crowd usually includes local busi-
ness people. It lends itself as the perfect spot to see and be
seen for an impressive and leisurely evening. *($$$)*

CYPRESS ROOM

(6000 N. Ocean Blvd. ☎ 843.449.6406 🖣 islandvista.com) The chef is well known and respected for his many years in some of the area's best restaurants. This is not a typical hotel dining room, but is an oceanfront restaurant with white linen service and a fresh creative menu. A big southern breakfast is cooked to order, and a gourmet (or kid-friendly) pizza menu is a good choice for lunch to go. For dinner, a starter of crispy-fried oysters or she crab soup is a delightful introduction to a beach visit. Featured items are the choice of sautéed, grilled, fried, or pan-blackened preparation for meat or fish entrées. The chef's specialties of rack of lamb or scallops are some of the best to be found. The extensive wine list offers appropriate pairings with any order. The dessert menu is equally creative and tempting with the traditional southern specialties of pecan pie or a fruit cobbler. Specialty beverages also provide some rich decadent treats for adult desserts. *($$$)*

DAGWOOD'S DELI

(400 11th Ave. N. ☎ 843.448.0100 or Dagwood's Deli & Sports Bar, 600 U.S. Hwy. 17 N., Surfside Beach ☎ 843.828.4600 🖣 dagwoodsdeli.com) The name implies big fat sandwiches and the deli does not disappoint, with tasty creations on fresh bread baked daily. The Myrtle Beach location has been a central downtown lunch spot for locals for many years, where it's common to see the uniformed staff from the fire and police department around the tables any day. It is sometimes closed during winter months. This company opened the neighboring **Bumstead's Pub** last year. The English-style pub offers an entrée and bar menu and boasts more than 150 beers in a fun atmosphere with late evening hours. The Surfside location offers flat-screen television in each of the 59 booths. *($)*

HARD ROCK CAFÉ

(1322 Celebrity Cir., Broadway at the Beach ☎ 843.946.0007 📱 hardrock.com) Music lovers cannot resist browsing the impressive collection of memorabilia on display. A traditional American menu and rock 'n roll music are both served with generous portions of fun in this restaurant, which has branches in 52 countries. Although it's a chain, each restaurant is unique and one-of-a-kind. The Myrtle Beach café is pyramid-shaped, with dazzling exterior lighting attracting the eye from a distance. Lunch and dinner are served daily from the Southern menu reflecting food items from the Memphis hometown of the founder. Legendary burgers, sandwiches such as the flying pig, salads and entrées are good and the experience even better. *($$)*

JIMMY BUFFETT'S MARGARITAVILLE

(1114 Celebrity Cir., Broadway at the Beach ☎ 843.448.5455 📱 margaritavillemyrtlebeach.com) The location offers a lake or street-front view, where the action is more interesting than the sister restaurant of **Cheeseburger in Paradise**. It's a "state of mind" featuring "Floribbean" fare which represents a combination of Florida influenced by the Caribbean. The frequent announcement of a hurricane party refers to the swirling hurricane on the ceiling which occasionally lowers a huge bottle of tequila for pouring into a gigantic mug. An entertaining display, to say the least. Suspended fish and airplanes are added to the décor for special interest. Boat drinks served in souvenir containers or any other beverage a party crowd desires are featured along with signature cheeseburgers and fresh seafood entrées. Specialties such as Coconut Shrimp or Jerk Salmon are typical fun fare for dining with the theme in mind. Mango and pineapple chunks plus candied walnuts added to a salad are more interesting than the big pile of chicken on top of it. Reservations are not accepted, but priority seating means that calling ahead may ensure seating. It's open for lunch and dinner daily. Jimmy Buffett is here occasionally, but don't count on it. Live entertainment performs on some weekends and daily during the summer season. *($$)*

LIBERTY STEAKHOUSE & BREWERY

(1321 Celebrity Cir., Broadway at the Beach ☎ 843.626.4677 ☗ libertysteakhouseandbrewery.com) The large bar area is often crowded with young people and business groups after work sampling the local microbrews which include new beer specialties to match the changing seasons. The spacious restaurant faces the lake, with the bar around the brewery facing additional outdoor seating on a patio. Appetizers such as the hot crab dip are tasty, and large entrées feature such popular American items as ribs and meatloaf. Lunch, dinner, and late night meals are served daily. *($$)*

LIBERTY TAP ROOM & GRILL

(7651 N. Kings Hwy. ☎ 843.839.4677 ☗ libertytaproom.com) Brews from the sister **Liberty Brewery** are offered in the large bar and restaurant, and a similar menu includes a wide variety of ribs, burgers, and pizzas. From small plates to big entrées and specialty homemade desserts, the dependable tastes are easy to appreciate. The bar area is filled with television screens and an outdoor area during the warm seasons. *($$)*

LONGBEARDS BAR & GRILL

(5040 Carolina Forest Blvd. ☎ 843.903.2905) Built and opened in late 2008, this is not along the traditional tourist route, although it is easy to spot from the drive into Myrtle Beach on

a distance, it appears to be a country dive or a
to frequent crowds of Harley Davidsons filling
 .... ɡ ..ɔt. The restaurant thinks of itself as a sportsman's
camp with game heads hanging from the fresh wood walls, but
it is actually a family-oriented restaurant with big menus for
breakfast, lunch, and dinner, and special game events as well
as regular Pittsburgh Steeler fan gatherings. As one of the only
restaurants serving quail, bison, and elk, along with plenty of
additional meats, poultry, and seafood, it's a refreshing visit
for any guest. Portions are large, beverages are plentiful, and
crowds comprise locals of all ages as well as visiting diners. *($)*

NEW YORK PRIME

(405 28th Ave., N. ☎ 843.448.8081 ✆ centraarchy.com) For an
upscale dinner or a he-man type of gathering, this fine restaurant emulates a Chicago-type steakhouse with a somewhat dark
masculine décor. Steaks are hand-cut at the table; everything
is à la carte with servings sized for two; cocktails and wine are
appropriately paired. Golfers are especially prone to choose
this fine restaurant. *($$$)*

P F CHANG'S

**(1100 Farrow Pkwy., The Market Common ☎ 843.839.9470
✆ pfchangs.com)** It is a chain restaurant found in many cities
such as Atlanta and Richmond, yet it's a favorite for lovers of
Chinese cuisine. International restaurants are not prominent
in the Myrtle Beach area. A widely varied menu featuring
many chicken, duck, and seafood dishes, large portions and
well-trained servers can please many diners. Bowls of soup
and lettuce wraps both deliver generous portions for two. It is
almost always extremely busy for dinner, especially on week-
ends. Reservations are recommended. *($$)*

PEACHES CORNER

(900 N. Ocean Blvd. ☎ 843.448.7424 🖱 peaches-corner.com) The
tradition of many Myrtle Beach visitors who have frequented
the central boulevard area since 1937 is to stop on the corner
where a bar stool beckons with a foot long hotdog and a big
frosty mug of beer. No one knows whether it's the tradition
or the foot long and brew which keeps this eatery busy year-
round. Beer is no longer sold for a dime, but the stools are still
filled beginning at 11:00 a.m. daily. *($)*

PIER 14 RESTAURANT & LOUNGE

(1306 Ocean Blvd. ☎ 843.448.4314 🖱 pier14.com) One of the
best panoramic views of the beach is showcased from this
windowed restaurant on the pier which was built in 1926. It's
nothing fancy, just a good, comfortable local choice. From the
street, it's hidden from view by the hotels in front of it. From
the beach, the pier is a central spot for fishing with swimmers
and sunbathers dotting the surrounding waters and sands.
Outside dining is a treat during most of the year. The restaurant usually closes for a month or two during December and
January, so it's wise to check in advance for the schedule. A fish
sandwich or fish entrée is always fresh, and seafood dinners
are popular. Live music and a full bar are a welcome backdrop
for casual gatherings on not most, but many evenings. See the
"Fishing" chapter for details about the pier. *($$)*

RIOZ BRAZILIAN STEAKHOUSE

(2920 Hollywood Dr. ☎ 843.839.0777 🖱 rioz.com) A Brazilian
steakhouse was the first of its kind in the Myrtle Beach area,
and has now been copied by similar smaller venues. For meat
lovers and big eaters, it's heaven on a hot skewer. The only

choices are either the salad bar or a meat dinner, with two price points. The salad bar includes hot vegetables, cold seafood salads, sushi, steamed shrimp, and all types of cold vegetable salad items, breads, and cheeses. The meats are served by *gauchos* (staff) continuously roaming the dining room with many different cuts and preparations of lamb, pork, beef, chicken, and sausages. A green coaster signals the waiter for service with *sim por favor* (yes, please) or *nao obragado* (no, thank you). Cocktails and desserts are not included in the cost of either of the unlimited buffets. Dinner is served daily. It's part of a 16-restaurant group located throughout Georgia, North, and South Carolina. *($$$)*

ROY & SID'S AMERICAN KITCHEN

(1160 Farrow Pkwy., The Market Common ☎ 843.839.9770 🖰 royandsids.com) An American menu in a casual family-friendly atmosphere is attractive within the popular center where shoppers are strolling the sidewalks and events are frequently presented in the common areas. Outdoor seating is a perfect place to celebrate an early spring lunch or dinner daily. Vegetables are especially popular here, as well as low carb and low cholesterol specialties which are not always the norm in this seafood-filled beach destination. The restaurant offers a Sunday brunch as well, and has a menu that includes several choices of big fat omelets accompanied by cheesy grits or hash browns and toast, pecan waffles, or blueberry pancakes. A chilled Bloody Mary or Mimosa nicely rounds out the brunch, especially when enjoyed on the patio during perfect spring or fall weather. *($$)*

RUTH'S CHRIS

(8761 Marina Pkwy. ☎ 843.838.9500 🖱 ruthschris.com) Part of a chain it may be, but it still is one of the top restaurants for upscale fine dining. Other South Carolina locations are Columbia and Greenville. New Orleans-inspired appetizers introduce signature steaks and chops. The food, presentation, and service are impeccable. The view of the Grand Dunes Marina makes this a good choice for a special occasion. Reservations are suggested to ensure a warm welcome or definitely for a large party. Dinner is served daily. *($$$)*

SEA CAPTAIN'S HOUSE

(3002 N. Ocean Blvd. ☎ 843.448.8082 🖱 seacaptains.com) A locally owned and traditional favorite of locals and visitors alike, this restaurant is in a central location and provides one of the best views in casual comfort with upscale cuisine. It's common to view dolphins splashing along the coast from the windowed dining room in the old oceanfront cottage. The chef is renowned for special seafood and dessert creations. The crowds are often waiting for breakfast, lunch or dinner, so calling ahead is recommended. *($$)*

SOHO CAFÉ AND BAR

(406 21st Ave. N. ☎ 843.443.9441 🖱 sohomyrtlebeach.com) For sushi and other seafood choices, or steaks, this is an informal choice, where young crowds gather around the bar for lunch or dinner until late night every day. From skewers to lo mein to hibachi or tempura, many preparations are offered, and fresh ingredients are key. It's somewhat dark and crowded, which creates the ambience of a lively happening spot. *($$)*

TBONZ GILL & GRILL

(1169 Seaboard St. ☎ 843.946.7111 and 4732 U.S. Hwy. 17 S.
North Myrtle Beach, Barefoot Landing ☎ 843.272.7111
⬤ tbonzgillandgrill.com) Two restaurants here are in the same
group as two in Charleston and two in Augusta, Georgia.
They do specialize in the gill and the grill, with steaks being
the predominant choice of most diners. Ribs are popular
here too. Other specialties are the she crab soup and the
cheese fries which are topped with ranch dressing and bits
of bacon as well as melted cheese. This choice would not be
on the low carbohydrate or low cholesterol diet list, but it's
a good option for splurging during a beach vacation. Lunch
and dinner are served daily. *($$)*

THE LIBRARY

(1212 N. Kings Hwy. ☎ 843.448.4527
⬤ thelibraryrestaurantsc.com) Everything about this upscale
restaurant is rare except its location. The mid-town business
location is not spectacular, so that its awning may be mistaken
for less than is expected. It has a three-star and *three diamond*
rating, with regular consumer reviews for excellence. With
tableside service in a dressy European and Continental atmo-
sphere, the Caesar salad, steak Diane, and flambéed dessert
offer a special meal for a romantic occasion. Chateaubriand or
Dover sole also are good choices which are not found in many
other local restaurants. This would not be suitable for children
or for dining in a rush. Dinner is served on all days except
Sundays. *($$$)*

THE MELTING POT

(5001 N. Kings. Hwy. ☎ 843.692.9003 🖰 meltingpot.com)
This fondue restaurant is consistently touted for its upscale, romantic ambience and fine cuisine. It's a good idea to make reservations and to choose this for a leisurely special occasion or with a lively group to share the dipping and sipping. It's a four-course experience, and the experience really is the key to enjoying this dinner. If you are in a rush or object to cooking steak or chicken at the table, this is not the best choice. Dinner is the only meal served. The special chocolate fondue can be sampled at occasional special events such as the annual Taste of the Town where the restaurant participates. *($$$)*

TOMMY BAHAMA'S RESTAURANT & BAR

(3044 Howard Ave., The Market Common ☎ 843.839.1868 🖰 tommybahama.com/cafe) Taste a little bit of Caribbean flavor with occasional island-inspired touches of coconut, mango, macadamia nut, or soy in delicious salad or seafood dishes. Sipping on a specialty mojito adds to the relaxing ambience with a view of the fountain and strolling shoppers. Patio dining in season is especially inviting for lunch or dinner. Shopping in the neighboring Tommy Bahama store is an added treat. *($$$)*

TRIPPS

(1311 Celebrity Cir., Broadway at the Beach ☎ 843.626.6455 🖰 trippsrestaurants.com) This chain has other restaurants, a couple in Virginia, and several in North Carolina where it originated. It's known for consistent quality and casual atmosphere. A fairly basic menu, the restaurant offers plenty of choices of burgers, steaks, chicken, seafood, and pasta, along with a full selection of sides and desserts. The bar is spacious and a good spot to grab a big, tasty salad or sandwich and a beer during a shopping excursion to this center. *($$)*

VILLA MARE RESTAURANT

(4999 Carolina Forest Blvd. ☎ 843.903.8654

🖱 **villamarerestaurant.com)** This true Italian restaurant has been one of the most popular local choices since 1990. It relocated to its current spot in 2008. It's open nightly except Sundays. Reservations are not required, but will be accepted. The owner greets guests at the door and remembers familiar faces forever. It's not dressy, but casual and comfortable. The pastas and veal dishes are among the best to be found. The crusty bread, salad, and homemade soup included with all entrées are always fresh. Regular diners lamented the loss of calzones which were a favorite at the previous location. *($$)*

Dining

RESTAURANT ROW RESTAURANTS

This is a local term for a strip slightly north of the Myrtle Beach city limit and south of North Myrtle Beach. It's been so called for its high concentration of a dozen or more restaurants within a couple of miles, and traffic is often judged by the congestion along this strip. No sign will denote Restaurant Row, but directions may be given with this designation. These restaurants are easily accessible from accommodations within Myrtle Beach and a short drive from North Myrtle Beach.

It is the location of two of the largest seafood buffet providers: **Bennett's Calabash Seafood** and **Original Benjamin's**. Each of these serves more than 100 items on a huge buffet with early-bird dinners beginning mid-afternoon. They are popular restaurants for tour groups traveling via bus and with some first-time visitors. The sheer quantities served in these demand bulk cooking rather than any individual attention to detail. Big eaters will find their fill. Discriminating diners expecting personal service and looking for unique entrées will not be happy at this type of large restaurant.

CAGNEY'S

(9911 U.S. 17 ☎ 843.449.0288 🖱 cagneysoldplace.com) Locally owned by Dino and his friend, also named Dino, who together also own **Flamingo**, this has been a landmark since 1976. The architecture, antiques, and salvaged woodwork used in the design of this large interesting building showcase their eclectic tastes. The Dancing Room often hosts entertainment, and returning guests gather around the bar to hash through the stories of their experiences here. Slow roasted prime rib is one of the specialties here; the steak menu is extensive and entrées are well prepared. Seafood lovers will be happy with the fresh catch of the day. It's open for dinner Monday through Saturday, but it usually closes for two months during the winter. *($$)*

CHESAPEAKE HOUSE

(9918 N. Kings Hwy. ☎ 843.449.3231
🖱 thechesapeakehouse.com) A special treat for diners here is the view of the lake crowded with turtles and an occasional alligator at the back of this restaurant. The homemade fragrant cinnamon rolls are among the best remembered elements of dinner here. The casual family-owned restaurant, operating since 1971, was the first restaurant to be built on what is now called Restaurant Row, the home of almost two dozen others. At first it was thought to be too far away

from Myrtle Beach. Now it's just barely outside the city limits and in the middle of a highly developed commercial section leading to the busy North Myrtle Beach. Fresh local seafood is featured. The fish stew, made from a family recipe of course, is a favorite starter with the baked flounder as an entrée for a healthy and delicious meal. Those who don't choose seafood are easily pleased with the southern fried chicken or steaks from the grill. Dinner is served every night, including an early-bird menu and group specials. Winter closing for two months is sometimes planned. *($$)*

CHESTNUT HILL

(9922 U.S. 17 N. ☎ 843.449.3984 ✇ chestnuthilldining.com) For Sunday brunch or nightly dinner, the seafood, beef, pasta, or veal are fresh and creative in a wide variety of preparations accompanied with homemade breads and desserts. Sunday brunch is a buffet with plenty of fresh, delicious choices of both, breakfast and lunch entrées. This is ideal for a big eater or for a family needing breakfast for some members and lunch for others. One of the best entrées for a seafood lover seeking a different item is the coquille which includes a combination of ingredients baked in a light sherry sauce in a puff pastry. Situated beside Chesapeake House, this restaurant is slightly dressier, although still casual. A view of the lake from the dining room or a gathering around the fireplace or bar is comfortable during cool weather. *($$)*

ROSSI'S

(9600 N. Kings Hwy. ☎ 843.449.0481 ✇ rossismyrtlebeach.com) A little bit upscale and with an established reputation for fine service and tasty Italian food, this is a good choice for a special meal with a group of friends. It's sometimes loud and crowded with fun-loving people. Reservations are a good idea during holidays or summer season due to the popularity of this spot. Fish, veal, and pastas are among the best for true Italian flavors. The bartenders know their business too and provide a welcoming spot when waiting for a table is required. It's open for dinner daily except Sundays. Adjoining is the **Eighty Eights** piano bar for after dinner socializing with dessert, coffee, or cordials and maybe a little bit of dancing. A children's menu is offered, but this is more suitable for adult dining. *($$)*

THOROUGHBRED'S

(9706 N. Kings Hwy. ☎ 843.497.2636

☎ **thoroughbredsrestaurant.com)** Long a favorite of golfers or romantics, this is one of the top of the list in the area's choices for an upscale dinner. It's a chophouse and seafood grill with a dim and private décor that showcases the white tablecloth service to perfect advantage. It's not a place for a quick meal. It's open daily for dinner and reservations are recommended. Steak lovers will find everything to their liking, although the Kentucky Derby portion of the menu offers poultry, veal, and lamb, while the Preakness section offers plenty of seafood items. Only the big eaters can make it to the home stretch for the famed Kentucky Derby pie. *($$$)*

NORTH STRAND RESTAURANTS

North Strand restaurant listings include Barefoot Landing and North Myrtle Beach. These restaurants, and dozens more not listed, are most convenient for visitors choosing accommodations in North Myrtle Beach.

BENNY RAPPA'S TRATTORIA

**(1453 U.S. Hwy. 17 S., North Myrtle Beach ☎ 843.361.1056
🖱 bennyrappas.com)** Benny and his wife are Italian owners who
create traditional specialties featuring fresh fish and pasta.
Everything is homemade, with authentic Italian recipes unique
in this area. A combination of lasagna and eggplant is a good
choice for someone who can't decide among the favorites.
Regular diners frequently request entrées which are not on the
menu, and are also likely to be accommodated. Tiramisu is
some of the best to be found, although most diners will need
to order the dessert to go. Be aware that the bread is an extra
charge, but it's definitely worth the extra buck or two. (Many
restaurants here serve bread, whether or not it's ordered.) This
is a fairly small menu in a small cozy restaurant, and it's not
really been discovered by visitors, so it can be easier to access
when better-known venues are full. *($$)*

CALIFORNIA DREAMING

**(10429 N. Kings Hwy. ☎ 843.663.2050 🖱 centraarchy.com/
californiadreaming.com)** A traditional American restaurant,
California Dreaming is part of the same group that owns
the **Carolina Roadhouse**. Additional ones in the chain are
also found in Charleston and Columbia, South Carolina,
and another one is located in south Myrtle Beach. The open
kitchen and consistent menu produce simple and tasty salads,
sandwiches, and entrées. The honey-drizzled croissant is a nice
touch, and is served with the house salad large enough for
many to enjoy as a basic lunch. *($$)*

CHERRY GROVE PIER

**(3500 N. Ocean Blvd., North Myrtle Beach ☎ 843.249.1625
🖱 cherrygrovepier.com)** Dining at any pier offers a spectacular view of the ocean, the fishing underway, and the surrounding beachfront activity. The view is often better than the food, but for an early breakfast, casual lunch, or an ice-cream stop, it can't be beat. This privately owned pier is a site in itself with its two-story observation deck at the end of the 985-foot pier. See the "Fishing" chapter for pier details. *($)*

GREG NORMAN'S AUSTRALIAN GRILLE

**(4930 U.S. 17 S., North Myrtle Beach ☎ 843.361.0000
🖱 shark.com/australiangrille)** The view and patio dining along the Intracoastal Waterway are probably the best part of this restaurant. Although a bit pricey, the selections and preparation are pleasing to diners expecting an upscale experience. Rack of lamb, wood-grilled seafood, steaks, duck, and many of the entrées are delicious. The adjoining bar is large and offers comfortable relaxation with the Greg Norman award-winning wines as a specialty. Lunch and dinner are served daily and the restaurant stays open on holidays as well. Reservations are suggested. *($$$)*

HOUSE OF BLUES

**(9922 U.S. 17 N., North Myrtle Beach ☎ 843.449.3984/
843.272.3000 🖱 houseofblues.com)** It is part of a 13-restaurant chain with similar menus, including several different "blues" burgers and entrées reflecting a few localized choices. Traditional New Orleans-influenced entrées are favorites, such as Creole Seafood Jambalaya and Cajun Meatloaf. Dining is casual and the portions are extremely large. Dining schedules

change occasionally with lunch and dinner served daily. A breakfast buffet and its one-of-a-kind Sunday Gospel Brunch are often featured during the summer. The Gospel Brunch is an excellent treat for dining while listening to uplifting music presented by a solo, trio, or traditional African-American choir. It's not Sunday church, but it lends inspiration along with entertainment and a big breakfast. This presentation is primarily offered during the busy season, so it's best to confirm before planning to dine here. The adjacent concert hall hosts big name entertainment in ticketed concerts, while the outdoor blues bar and the restaurant often present free live music, dance floors, and plenty of fun for happy people gathered around two bars. See the "Entertainment" chapter for details of the concert hall. *($$)*

ROCKEFELLER'S RAW BAR

(3614 Hwy. 17 S., North Myrtle Beach ☎ 843.361.9677 ● rockefellersrawbar.com) For lunch, happy hour or late night choices from the raw bar menu or steam pot of shellfish, this extremely casual local restaurant is a popular choice. This is a no-frills eatery, although the plastic palm trees might be considered a bit frilly! Several televisions lend the atmosphere of a sports bar, and the friendly staff does a good job of welcoming a loud crowd of golfers along with neighborhood folks. *($)*

UMBERTO'S

(4886 S. Kings Hwy., North Myrtle Beach ☎ 843.272.1176 ● umbertos.com) Pittsburgh Italian Trattoria is the description the owner prefers. Homemade bread and family style beans, salad, and pasta are famous accompaniments for every entrée.

The gigantic chops, steak or osso bucco are large enough for two, although an extra charge may be applied for sharing. Expect to find big groups of loud golfers and happy people having a good time over bottles of house wine and traditional pasta dishes also. It's an experience as well as a fine meal. Reservations are suggested. *($$)*

SOUTH STRAND RESTAURANTS

South Strand restaurants are in Pawleys Island, Murrells Inlet, Surfside, and Garden City. They are convenient for visitors choosing accommodations on the South Strand. Although an easy drive from the central section of Myrtle Beach, daily dining on the South Strand is not recommended unless staying in this area.

BISTRO 217

(10707 U.S. Hwy. 17, Pawleys Island ☎ 843.235.8217 ● bistro217.com) It's a casual choice for locals to drop in for lunch, although a bit pricey for salads and sandwiches, or the $12 hotdog. Fish tacos and quiche are nice choices. People who love a fish taco tend to rank all the restaurants they visit by this item, and this is in the running for number one with most judges. For a dinner starter, calamari lovers will be happy with the giant fried offer including interesting pepper sauces and an aioli. For an entrée the pork schnitzel or the eggplant specialty are quite different from most items on other local menus. Who would have thought of adding the favorite shrimp, scallops, and grouper to the general concept of eggplant parmesan? Availability of outdoor seating and occasional live entertainment add to the ambience of this as a gathering spot during good weather. *($$)*

BOVINE'S

(3979 U.S. 17 Bus., Murrells Inlet ☎ 843.651.2888
🖱 **divinedininggroup.com)** Wood-fired specialties of steak,
seafood, or ribs include some southwest touches and are
accompanied by an extensive wine list. Diners who love a large
steak are probably in the right place here, although seafood
is fine as well. The cornbread and the corn pudding have a
little bit of a country flavor and are worth rave reviews. A
rustic, longhorn appearance overlooks the scenic inlet with
unmatched sunset views. Dinner is the only meal, and it can be
expected to be crowded during the summer season. *($$)*

DIVINE FISH HOUSE

(3993 U.S. 17 Bus., Murrells Inlet ☎ 843.651.5800
🖱 **divinefishhouse.com)** The dining deck and tiki bar overlooking
the inlet and its scenic marsh are special locations for seasonal
dining, but indoor meals are equally scenic. The sushi bar
stays busy, and the seafood creations from the grill or oven are
dependably well-prepared. The restaurant also hosts occasional
live entertainment. Dinner is the only meal here, and it is often
busy during the middle of summer. *($$)*

DRUNKEN JACK'S

(4031 U.S. 17 Bus., Murrells Inlet ☎ 843.651.3232
🖱 **drunkenjacks.com)** Legend holds that Jack was a drunken
crewman left behind when Blackbeard's remaining crew
sailed. The view of the inlet and Snug Harbor Marina are
spectacular from the restaurant and the open deck. The large
menu features seafood, meat, and chicken for dinner daily.
Sandwiches and seafood are the choices for lunch every day
except Mondays. Live entertainment appears during summer

evenings and on some weekends year-round. As with most restaurants in Murrells Inlet during the summer, a wait may be expected for seating. *($$)*

HOT FISH CLUB

(4911 U.S. 17 Bus., Murrells Inlet ☎ 843.651.3197
☗ **hotfishclub.com)** The Hot and Hot Fish club was the legendary first restaurant which has now grown into dozens of places to eat in the inlet. In the late 1800s, it was a clubhouse on a small island near here. Today's restaurant appears rustic, although the fine wine list and the beautifully prepared entrées suit today's refined tastes for seafood. The view of the inlet is one of the best parts of dining here. Dinner is served Wednesday through Sunday, and the neighboring Gazebo offers the full restaurant menu. The lively entertainment in the gazebo is frequent, with special events and lots of dancing to celebrate certain special occasions, such things as John Lennon's birthday. *($$)*

FLO'S PLACE

(3797 U.S. 17 Bus., Murrells Inlet ☎ 843.651.7222
☗ **flosplace.com)** It's a fun place with a deck hanging off the back over the creek. It has a New Orleans menu and atmosphere reminiscent of Flo's childhood in the bayou. It's the only local restaurant which serves alligator in a stew or in an appetizer. It will be an imported meat from a farm and not one of the critters which might occasionally slide along the creek below. The red beans and rice are as good as any served in New Orleans too. A steam pot is a specialty, and sharing a pot is part of the fun if you like to suck the crawfish, shuck the oysters, or shell the shrimp. For lunch the big, fat bun filled

with fried seafood is a traditional PoBoy, which demands a touch of green sauce. Careful that it's a touch, not a splash, of sauce too, remembering that green may be spicier than red. *($$)*

GULFSTREAM CAFÉ

(1536 S. Waccamaw Dr., Garden City ☎ 843.651.8808 ▢ centraarchy.com) The view of the ocean or the inlet are one-of-a-kind from this restaurant, and the menu for Sunday brunch or dinner are in keeping with the atmosphere of visiting the south end of the beach. The Lowcountry Sunday brunch menu is unmatched, beginning with a Sunrise Cocktail or a Bloody Caesar and proceeding to seafood crêpes or a Lowcountry Benedict. If seafood doesn't suit for brunch, the huge steak and eggs entrée will please those with large appetites. Other creative, delicious choices are served with several varieties of coffee or cocktail recipes.

Sunsets are unlike any other place and displayed in all their glory here. Summer brings music on the deck and huge crowds. Don't be in a rush, and enjoy the experience. The she crab soup is always a favorite, and steak lovers enjoy the filet medallions. Early-bird specials are quite a deal too. The restaurant group includes **New York Prime**, **California Dreaming**, and **Carolina Roadhouse**; all are consistent quality. *($$$)*

NIBILES RESTAURANT AT SURFSIDE PIER

(11 S. Ocean Blvd., Surfside Beach ☎ 843.238.5080) It's a favorite for breakfast such as a seafood omelet, or for she crab soup which is one of the specialties as a starter or entrée for lunch or dinner. The family-owned restaurant which has been a visitor favorite for many years offers an outstanding view of the beach. The décor is a dated early beach look which is part of its tradition. Visitors from New York and Ohio return on each trip, and the staff recognizes many familiar faces. *($)*

OLIVER'S LODGE

(4204 U.S. Hwy. 17 Bus., Murrells Inlet ☎ 843.851.1139 🖱 oliverslodgerestaurant.com) This claims to be the oldest restaurant on the entire Grand Strand. The original part of the structure was a summer beach home built by the state's lieutenant governor in the 1860s. It became a lodge in 1910. The second generation of owners began offering a menu in 1947. Its storied history includes hosting the wedding of famed crime novelist, Mickey Spillane in 1983 and one of his last birthday parties before his death in 2006. Current owners have renovated to enhance the house. The view of the inlet is spectacular. Fresh fish would be a good bet, as the boats are almost in view where it arrives. *($$)*

LITTLE RIVER RESTAURANTS

Little River is on the river where a few typical seafood dives offer fresh local catches and scenic views. They appear to be authentic dives, such as **Key West Crazy, Pilot House,** and **Fibber's on the Water**, although they are acceptable options to many visitors looking to grab a fish sandwich and a beer. **Capt. Juel's Hurricane Restaurant** offers table service and great views of the water. These are not listed and reviewed separately here, as they are not likely choices for dining, but they can be easily found when in the village.

The best time to really see and sample the flavor of Little River and the restaurant offerings is during an annual festival such as the **Blue Crab Festival** in mid-May or the **Shrimp** and **Jazz Festival** in mid-October. See the "Events" chapter for details. The **gambling boats** depart from here and also lead visitors to an overview of the little village. See the "Attractions" chapter for details.

It's easy to be unaware of the river view on a drive through the main commercial strip which is U.S. Hwy. 17, the route between Wilmington and Myrtle Beach. This drive has no view of the river and appears so packed with a mixture of businesses, bars, and fast food that it would be easy to miss seeing the few really fine non-traditional restaurants which are tucked away among the jumble. Wine connoisseurs will be delighted with these rare finds, as will discerning diners seeking Italian, French, or Southern influences in leisurely dinners.

CHIANTI SOUTH ITALIAN RESTAURANT

(2109 Hwy. 17 N., Little River ☎ 843.249.7888 🖱 Chianti.us) Northern Italian cuisine distinguishes this gracious restaurant. It is the first and only local recipient of *Wine Spectator's* award of excellence every year since opening in 1998. The owners Angelo and Marie Bertolozzi previously operated their Chianti Restaurant in Newburgh, NY, for 17 years. Old and new traditional Italian recipes grace the seafood, pasta, and meat dishes. Don't forget the dolci (desserts) such as the award-winning Tiramisu Casalingo or the Profiterolle Al Cioccoloto which is the ultimate filled homemade pastry puff. *($$)*

PARSON'S TABLE

(4305 McCorsley Ave., Little River ☎ 843.249.3702 🖱 parsonstable.com) It's been awarded a *Three diamond* from *AAA*, a six-year *Wine Spectator* award of excellence, and recognized by *Wine Enthusiast* magazine. The chef has been named one of the best in the country. However, it seems to be a very well kept secret if you venture forth without a recommendation and directions. The restaurant exterior looks like a church, which was, interestingly, its original use. The antique stained glass, beveled glass, flooring, and heavy doors came from other churches and a farm house. The restaurant faces a side street, although it's easily accessible from U.S. Hwy. 17 which is the main route between Wilmington and Myrtle Beach. Several good steak choices are offered, and the seafood is especially good with sautéed grouper, stuffed flounder, or a shrimp dish to please the discriminating palate. The recommended wine is paired with each entrée. The bacon-wrapped shrimp is a unique tasty appetizer, and the she crab soup is rich and authentic. The respectable beer selection includes non-alcoholic choices, and the coffee is gourmet. In spite of the recognition and the impressive menu, it's not an intimidating dining experience; yet it should be savored and not rushed. Dinner is served daily except Sunday and Monday. Brunch is a special event on Sundays, with an especially interesting menu, including such delights as Crab Cake Benedict, shrimp and grits, or steak and eggs. Early bird and happy hour specials are offered, along with petite servings of some entrées. (*$$*)

THE BRENTWOOD RESTAURANT & WINE BAR
(4269 Luck Ave., Little River ☎ 843.249.2601

🖱 thebrentwoodrestaurant.com) Yet another restaurant that will not be noticed without a recommendation, this is a lovely, upscale, classical restaurant in a restored circa 1910 home. It's visible from U.S. Hwy. 17, although it sits back from the highway and faces a side street. Except on Sundays, the restaurant is usually open for happy hour and dinner. It's

ajor holidays and is a nice choice for a special

bar on weekends offers a special treat with

s, local resident with New York experience and

an impressive recording career. The mood is enhanced by the architecture and the seating in different rooms, as if it's still a private home hosting a few guests for dinner. Choose from a light menu at the upstairs wine bar, early bird three-course specials, a four-course *prix fixe* (fixed price) or a diverse *les viandes* (meats) and *les poissons* and *fruits de mer* (seafood) menu. The French chef/owner, Eric Masson, has classical training and extensive experience, which is reflected in the delicious and creative entrées, such as seafood bouillabaisse or poached salmon. This is one local place that does not serve a fried seafood platter. The discriminating seafood lover will be happy with the royal platter which is large and pricey but worth it. *($$$)*

SNOOKY'S

(4495 Baker St., Little River ☎ 843.249.5252

🖱 **snookysonthewater.com)** Waterway and marina views from the deck of this clean, crisp eatery are the reason to bring a camera and think about arriving for "docktail" hour. Yes, the dock is right here and the cocktails pair perfectly with sunsets over the water. This is a secret find which is not on a main route other than the water, but it's gradually finding its way into the minds – and palates – of the local community. The amazing food is the reason to plan lunch or dinner here any day. Chef George Elefantis was the protégé of Chef Jeff Burr who opened this restaurant and is known for his tradition at West Virginia's famed Greenbrier. A seafood pasta or daily special is recommended, although the fried grouper bites and fried green tomato baguette are also irresistible. *($$)*

PAT & MIKE'S IRISH PUB

(1359 U.S. Hwy. 17, Little River ☎ 843.249.7145 ☻ patandmikesirishpub.com) Lunch and dinner are served daily, and late night crowds frequent the bar for local entertainment, karaoke, or football on television with a pint or two. Fish and chips are as good as can be found. Most entrées are more American than Irish, but the big sandwiches, big salads, and entrées are tasty. Although the décor is somewhat dated, the view over the lake and golf course is attractive. *($$)*

CALABASH RESTAURANTS

This fishing village is the southernmost community in North Carolina, just a minute off the main route from Wilmington to Myrtle Beach. It's easy to access for a seafood meal, although likely to be crowded during the peak of summer season. A dozen or more restaurants are within a couple of miles here. The following recommendations are dependable favorites.

CAPTAIN JOHN'S SEAFOOD HOUSE

(8998 Nance St., Calabash, NC ☎ 910.579.6011) The fishing boats are docked right here, and the food couldn't be any fresher or the view more authentic. A buffet is usually offered, but entrées on the menu lend more choices for diners seeking baked or broiled dinners rather than the typically fried meals. The stuffed flounder is a favorite, and it's one of the best places to eat hush puppies although they may be ubiquitous among all seafood restaurants. It closes during the winter and boasts long lines during the summer, so a fall or spring visit is a convenient time to dine here if the opportunity presents itself. *($$)*

CALABASH SEAFOOD HUT

(1125 River Rd., Calabash, NC ☎ 910.579.6723) Created from a fast-food joint, it usually has a line standing at the window or sitting on outdoor benches, waiting to order or waiting to pick up. It's tiny, but seating is available with a wait for a table on most days. Nothing fancy, no silver or china and definitely no white linen, this is one of the most popular of the dives to be found on the coast. Although appearing to be a dive, its cleanliness is not questionable. It's been a family-owned tradition for many years. Fried fish, shrimp, scallops, crab cakes, or oysters are among the specialties. It's open year-round for lunch and dinner except for Mondays. *($)*

THE GRAPEVINE RESTAURANT

(9991 Beach Dr., Calabash, NC ☎ 910.575.6565) When visitors have had their fill of fried seafood, this is a welcome choice. It's not typical of Calabash. Seafood is offered, but it is usually baked with creative sauces rather than fried, and other entrées are attractive options as well. Pastas are good and the bread is homemade. The daily special is always a good idea. Locals gather around the bar, and entertainment is sometimes a treat. *($$)*

CONWAY RESTAURANTS

Conway is a quaint little river town which has captured its historic charm in a few shops and restaurants in the downtown business district where the county government is also located. Although most visitors to the beach area do not stay here, it's worth a visit for a meal and stroll through historic areas. See the "Events" and "Attractions" chapters for details about a few things to do here, and if interested in staying here, see the "Lodging" chapter for bed-and-breakfast listings.

THE TRESTLE BAKERY & CAFÉ

(308 Main St., Conway ☎ 843.248.9896

🖰 trestlebakery.com) The bakery is a few doors down the street for ordering wedding cakes and specialty items. Café dining is popular here for breakfast or lunch, and it may be tough to find a table. Varying hot specials include tasty plates as fried chicken, meatloaf, pot roast, and a creative cheeseburger quiche. Wonderful homemade soups such as loaded potato or sweet corn-crab chowder are offered daily. Specialty salads are several varieties of preparations with chicken, shrimp, or tuna and can be purchased by the pound as well as on a sandwich or platter. Sandwiches are a mile high on thick fresh homemade sourdough bread. The shelves are filled with collectibles from early farm life and country kitchens. A selection of canned gift items such as pepper jam, black bean salsa, and peanut butter schmeer are also stacked. *($$)*

RIVERTOWN BISTRO

(1111 Third Ave., Conway ☎ 843.248.3733

🖰 RivertownBistro.com) Both lunch and supper – dinner is referred to as supper here – are delicious with a casual ambience. As well as a diverse menu, the Blue Plate Specials tempt the taste buds with economical offers ranging from meatloaf to slow roasted port pot roast, and seafood. It's all homemade and popular with folks who live around the corner as well as those who will drive 30 minutes for a special dinner. The appearance is early river town, but the dining is better than anything expected in a bistro with a small-town atmosphere. *($$)*

There are more than 7,000 camp sites in the area, and Myrtle Beach has often been referred to as "The Campground Capital of the World."

Lodging

★

Myrtle Beach's first hotel was the Seaside Inn, built in 1901. In the early days, $2 would buy three meals and an overnight stay, and at first, the hotel had no plumbing or electricity. Times have changed since the Seaside Inn was demolished in the late 1920s.

Accommodations are plentiful in the Myrtle Beach area. Hotels, villas, and condos together offer more than 90,000 sleeping rooms. Additionally, hundreds of rental houses are offered, and campgrounds appeal to many visitors. Advance reservations are recommended, definitely during the prime season between Memorial Day and Labor Day. Special events during the winter off season or spring and fall seasons can also create high occupancy particularly in the specific areas of an event.

Rates typically are at the peak on July 4 and are as little as half the amount in mid-winter. Fall and winter specials are common and are ideal choices for travelers who can set their own schedule to take advantage of value packages. Rates are not quoted here due to the wide fluctuation from one week or one season to another and from one year to the next. The high-end properties are designated as luxury, and all others suggested here are considered moderate mid-range.

Tipping for maid service at accommodations is neither expected nor required, but it is a nice courtesy to leave a few dollars on the day of check-out.

Beachfront hotels or rental houses within easy walking distance to the beach are choice lodging for families with children to en-

Lodging

tertain. Visitors seeking the evening sound of crashing waves or the morning wakeup call of sunrise over the ocean will also be interested in beachfront or beach view accommodations which are available in abundance.

Golfers are typically occupied navigating the greens rather than the beach during the day and may choose golf villas or condo rental units to accommodate a foursome or more. Several of these are within the golf resorts rather than on the beachfront. Many hotels do offer golf packages, and additional rentals specialize in providing convenient access to several courses.

Whether planning for a golf outing, a family vacation, a romantic escape, or attending a business or entertainment event, discussing the location is advisable when making reservations. Proximity to the preferred activities is not a problem. Many of the hotels are owned by family groups or managed in a collective and are happy to recommend the most suitable of their group to please the guest.

CAMPGROUNDS

Camping in the Myrtle Beach area is popular for families and groups and for snowbirds. They are also sometimes the preference for discretionary spending rather than more expensive accommodations. Many choose to stay for a month or more to escape the cold winters of the northern United States or while navigating between north and south on an annual trek to Florida. Campgrounds are well equipped and easily accessible from any part of the area, as well as conveniently placed for restaurants, attractions, and entertainment. More than 7,000 campsites are in the area.

APACHE FAMILY CAMPGROUND

(9700 Kings Rd. ☎ 843.449.7323

⛺ apachefamilycampground.com) This campground at the ocean-front offers beach sites and wooded sites. It is equipped with everything the camper needs, including campsites for RVs or rental units and golf cart rentals. A fishing pier lures anglers to live here for a longer period. A playground, store, restaurant, dominoes, regular entertainment, and worship services are further reasons for the popularity of Apache. It's clean and well maintained.

HUNTINGTON BEACH STATE PARK

(16148 Ocean Hwy., Murrells Inlet ☎ 843.237.4440/ 1-866-345-7275 ⛺ huntingtonbeachsc.org) This is in Georgetown County, but easily accessible at the south of Myrtle Beach and a popular site, as are all South Carolina parks. Two campgrounds near the beach provide 107 sites with electricity and water; 24 additional sites include sewer; another six walk-in tent sites include tent pads. All are near hot showers and restrooms. Birders and nature lovers will enjoy the maritime forest and the three-mile beach. The state's toll free number is recommended for advance camping reservations, although local information would be available at the park office.

MYRTLE BEACH STATE PARK

(4401 S. Kings Hwy. ☎ 843.238.5325

⛺ myrtlebeachstatepark.net) As well as campsites, five cabins and two apartments are available. They are fully furnished and fitted out with essential amenities, but somewhat primitive, as might be expected in a state park. Campsites for RVs with electricity and water total 302. Forty-five tent sites with access to central water are available for summer only. Free wireless Internet is available. A camp store provides limited supplies and firewood. Store and office hours vary with the seasons. Dump station and laundry facilities are available, as well as restrooms and hot showers. A two-night minimum is required, and advance reservations are recommended. The state's toll free number is preferred for advance camping reservations.

OCEAN LAKES FAMILY CAMPGROUND

(6001 S. Kings Hwy. ☎ 843.239.5636 ✆ oceanlakes.com) This campground is so good that it was named National RV Park of the Year by the national organization. It includes 900 campsites which are oceanfront, lakeside, or shaded. There are 300 rental houses throughout the campground, which are a variety of mobile homes and beach cottages. Amenities include a pool, game center, mini-golf course, laundry, Internet access, and entertainment is offered regularly.

PIRATELAND FAMILY CAMPING RESORT

(5401 S. Kings Hwy. ☎ 843.238.5155 ✆ pirateland.com) The family campground offers 1,500 sites with a heated indoor pool, lazy river, and spacious beach front. Miniature golf and supervised children's activities are offered seasonally. Laundry and Internet access plus golf cart rentals and golf course discounts are available.

HOTELS AND CONDOS

Hotels, timeshares, and condos cannot always be distinguished from each other by their appearance, unless it's the amenities and services that may be different. Accommodations are recommended in a few of the most upscale and many which are general mid-range properties. The majority of these are locally owned. Additional chain hotels are available and can be found through an easy Internet search if a specific brand is preferred. The ocean-front hotels or condos are recommended, as the majority of visitors are looking for the beach as the main attraction. Dozens of additional hotels and motels beyond these suggestions may please some guests. Many in the central Myrtle Beach area are second or third row with an easy walk to the beach, but few amenities.

LUXURY ACCOMMODATIONS

The Myrtle Beach area overall is not considered a luxury destination, although the few noted as such are suitable for the most discriminating taste.

LITCHFIELD PLANTATION
(99 Gathering Ln., Litchfield ☎ 843.237.9121
litchfieldplantation.com) This historic inn is a rare find for the discriminating traveler who is not looking for family beach hotels with lazy rivers. It's situated well away from any hustle and bustle of the beach area, yet dining and entertainment are accessible. It's located on a 250-year-old plantation on a real river and is bordered by 600 acres of live oak trees, marshland and remnants of the rice culture of the South Carolina lowcountry. The charm of bygone days is introduced with the drive through moss-draped live oaks, and the setting affords new memories for wedding parties or corporate retreats. Four luxurious private suites are located in the plantation house. An additional 15 unique guest rooms are in nearby cottages and villas. Hot breakfast is included, and private dining at the

Carriage House Club restaurant is available. Tennis courts and an outdoor pool are on the property. A private marina with boat moorage on the property and a beach house on Pawleys Island are available. Package specials are offered for weddings, honeymoons, or other special occasion.

MARINA INN

(1499 Grande Dunes Blvd., Myrtle Beach ☎ 843.913.1333
☻ **marinainnatgrandedunes.com)** One of the newest hotels in the area is a *AAA Four Diamond* property offering 200 rooms and suites with Intracoastal Waterway views from each. Rooms are spacious and amenities are upscale. The hotel overlooks the full service marina which has watercraft rentals. An oceanfront cabana beach club is available for access to the beach. Tennis and golf are offered in the member clubs. A café, lounge, and restaurant are conveniently located within the hotel, and **Ruth's Chris** is a short walk away along the marina walk. It's a business hotel with comfortable meeting rooms and would not be a likely choice for a family beach vacation. Several packages include those designed for family, holidays, romance, or an off season combination. One offer packages golf, entertainment, and a visit to **Brookgreen Gardens** which is the area's most spectacular art attraction. See the "Attractions" chapter for description.

MARRIOTT MYRTLE BEACH RESORT

(800 Costa Verde Dr., Myrtle Beach ☎ 843.449.8880
☻ **marriottmyrtlebeachresort.com)** This property on the ocean-front opened in 2005 and is designated *AAA Four Diamond*, especially suitable for business travelers but also great for family vacations. The location is convenient, but not in the middle of the busiest section. Eight ocean view suites and 400

guest rooms are tasteful and comfortable. Its amenities and location make it a popular choice for business meetings. It's highly rated by travel magazine readers as a golf resort, and also for the excellent spa and all-round amenities. Swimming options are indoor and outdoor pools, a water slide, and of course the ocean. A unique breakfast package or a resort credit package occasionally is available. Golf, tennis, and a fitness center at the Grande Dunes are available.

SHERATON MYRTLE BEACH CONVENTION CENTER HOTEL

(2101 N. Oak St., Myrtle Beach ☎ 843.918.5000 starwoodhotels.com) Adjoining the Myrtle Beach Convention Center and comprising 402 rooms, junior suites, executive suites, club suites, and a presidential suite, this is an ideal business traveler's choice. The convenient location is ten minutes away from the airport by cab or rental car, a walkable two blocks west of the beach, and a quick drive from **Broadway at the Beach** or **Coastal Grande Mall** for shopping and dining. It was awarded *AAA's Three Diamond* status in 2008. A full-service restaurant, bar, and coffee shop are convenient. Completely smoke free, this hotel offers an indoor pool, sun deck, and state-of-the-art fitness facility. It is also a comfortable option for families who may accompany a business traveler.

CENTRAL MYRTLE BEACH ACCOMMODATIONS

The city address of all of these is Myrtle Beach. They are within the city limits and are most convenient for visitors choosing a wide variety of family attractions.

ANDERSON OCEAN CLUB

(2600 N. Ocean Blvd. ☎ 843.213.5370 🖱 oceanaresorts.com)
This new condo property is on the beach in a central location, convenient to the Myrtle Beach Convention Center for travelers who might include families on business trips. The large one-, two- and three-room units and terrific views are popular. Indoor and outdoor pools, lazy river, and seasonal oceanfront pool bar and large sundeck provide the favorite time away from the business center. The full-service day spa, along with the hair-and-nail salon offer special treats. Off season and holiday specials are attractively priced, as are the golf packages with many options. Senior and military discounts are also offered.

BEACH COLONY

(5308 N. Ocean Blvd. ☎ 843.449.4010 🖱 beachcolony.com) Most of the rooms are oceanfront or with an angled ocean view, with choice of one-bedroom studio or one-, two-, three- or four-bedroom condos. Outdoor pools are heated, and the lazy river lends drifting pleasure for children, while the sauna and indoor pool, and whirlpool also provide year-round comfort. Racket ball, shuffleboard, and the exercise room lead energetic travelers away from the pool bar and oceanfront lounge. Special offers include packages with breakfast, romance, off season, holiday, military, or monthly stays plus economy golf packages. Groups of 100 to 200 persons may be accommodated for meetings.

THE BREAKERS RESORT

(Oceanfront at 21st Ave. N. ☎ 843.444.4444 🖱 breakers.com) A traditional oceanfront hotel, the Breakers Resort offers one-, two- and three-bedroom condos. The newer, adjacent tower has condos which are equipped with all possible amenities. Indoor and outdoor pools, plus a lazy river and interactive pirate adventure on the water add to the interest for families with children. A coffee shop, bar, and restaurant are across the street. This has its own meeting facilities for up to 200 persons and is a three-block walk to the Myrtle Beach Convention Center. Golf or entertainment packages and off season specials are offered.

CAMELOT BY THE SEA

(2000 N. Ocean Blvd. ☎ 843.916.4700 🔋 camelotresort.com)
The only themed resort hotel in the area, this attractive hotel offers oceanfront suites with balconies, Roman spas, pools – inside and outside – lazy river, and business facilities. It's conveniently located near restaurants and coffee shops. Monthly and weekly rates are offered.

CAPTAIN'S QUARTERS RESORT

(901 S. Ocean Blvd. ☎ 843.448.1404 🔋 captainsquarters.com)
Oceanfront, ocean view or interior rooms, suites, efficiencies with cooking facilities in the room and apartments are offered in the oceanfront building. The hotel has a total of 15 indoor and outdoor pools, and a water attraction and lazy rivers both in and outdoors. The 20-lane bowling center and arcade are the top amenities here for families. Plenty of pool deck space, a seasonal pool bar, and grill round out the leisure space. The breakfast restaurant on the top floor displays a spectacular view of the beachfront. Off-season and holiday specials offer attractive rates.

CARAVELLE RESORT

(6900 N. Ocean Blvd. ☎ 843.918.8000 ✆ thecaravelle.com)
Oceanfront, ocean view, or terrace view suites and efficiencies are located in the 15-story oceanfront building with 540 units renovated in 2007. Additional buildings on the property offer condos. The breakfast buffet is popular, and family night dinners are served seasonally. The outdoor poolscape stretches for an entire block along the oceanfront, and the indoor heated pool, fitness, and game rooms provide plenty of space for recreation and relaxation. Off season specials add free nights or breakfast to several packages. Custom golf packages are of interest to serious players who can choose their preferred upscale courses. Conference and banquet space are attractive for group or wedding events.

CARIBBEAN RESORT & VILLAS

(3000 N. Ocean Blvd. ☎ 843.448.7181 ✆ caribbeanresort.com)
The main oceanfront resort offers oceanfront or angled-view suites and condos with up to four bedrooms. It's conveniently located for business, golf or family travel. Indoor and outdoor splash pools and a lazy river provide enough water to entertain all ages. A large part of the charm in this stay is the fine oceanfront dining at **Sea Captain's House** next door. Details are in the "Dining" chapter. The experienced golf department can provide a package to meet any request. Family or romantic-escape packages are offered. Special rates for last minute or early booking, off season, free nights, free breakfast or senior rates are also offered.

CORAL BEACH

(1105 S. Ocean Blvd. ☎ 843.448.8421 🖱 thecoralbeach.com)
This is a good family or group accommodation for any time of year due to its size and recreational amenities. It's a large property in a nice location slightly south of the busiest part of the beach. It offers ten pools indoors and out, a lazy river, and a large arcade area. A water park was added in 2009. The additional surprise is an eight-lane bowling alley in the hotel. The restaurant features entertainment during the summer season. Holiday and fall specials are promoted at great rates. Rooms are somewhat dated, although not atypical for the location.

CROWN REEF

(2913 S. Ocean Blvd. ☎ 843.626.8077 🖱 crownreef.com) When glimpsed at night, the Crown Reef's night spotlights make the hotel's buildings appear purple. All the 514 guest rooms, suites, and efficiencies are oceanfront with private balconies. Pools also face the ocean and the lazy river promises to be the largest in town. Two restaurants and a lounge are on-site. Conference facilities accommodate up to 1,200 persons. Wedding planning and golf packages are offered. Although not in the middle of the busiest strip, it is convenient to the entire beach area.

DUNES VILLAGE

(5200 N. Ocean Blvd. ☎ 843.449.5275 🖱 dunesvillage.com) A huge indoor water park including an adult water slide, water volleyball, and basketball, is a major attraction for families who enjoyed this accommodation for many years before its transformation into a type of entertainment complex. Oceanfront or angled-view units range from studio rooms up to four-bedroom. Rates are low during the off season, and a wide variety of package choices include entertainment or attractions. A large number of golf packages provide many choices of courses. Military, veteran, and senior citizen rates are suggested.

EMBASSY SUITES HOTEL

(9800 Lake Dr. or 9800 Queensway Blvd. ☎ 843.449.0006 🖰 embassysuites.com) This is a wonderful location within Kingston Plantation, located north of Myrtle Beach and south of North Myrtle Beach and convenient to all business, golf, or entertainment. The recently renovated 255 oceanfront suites are spacious. Bicycle rentals, fitness, tennis, racket ball, jogging track, and pool are all on-site. All business services are available. The adjacent conference and banquet facility can accommodate more than 1,000 persons for meetings or weddings. Eating options range from a complimentary breakfast buffet to the ocean-view grill, which is open for breakfast and lunch. For dinner, guests can head to the **Omaha Steakhouse.**

FOREST DUNES

(5511 N. Ocean Blvd. ☎ 843.449.0864 🖰 forestdunes.com) Oceanfront or ocean view suites or condos up to three-bedroom are in a beautiful oceanfront location. Full kitchens are included in all units, and extended stays are encouraged. Indoor and outdoor pools, lazy river and game room are convenient. The jogging trail along the oceanfront is one of the best in the area for spectacular displays of sunrise or sunset without obstruction. Monthly rates or free nights are especially attractive off season offers. Military and senior rates also are available.

HILTON MYRTLE BEACH RESORT

(10000 Beach Club Dr. ☎ 843.449.6000 🖱 hilton.com) This oceanfront property within Kingston Plantation offers 385 oceanfront or ocean-view rooms or suites. A perfect place for golfing enthusiasts, the property also includes the **Arcadian Shores Golf Course** and the **Hilton Golf Academy**. The outdoor pool is oceanfront. The nearby sports and health club houses an indoor pool and also offers massage therapy services. Business events are convenient in the conference facilities, and the oceanfront ballroom is an ideal location for special events such as weddings. The hotel offers tennis and golf packages for interested guests.

ISLAND VISTA RESORT

(6000 N. Ocean Blvd. ☎ 843.449.6406 🖱 islandvista.com) This 12-story property offers 149 rooms on one of the preferred sections of beachfront. It opened in 2006 on the site of the former Sea Island Inn. Visitors who remember the quality it offered will be pleased with the all-suite replacement offering rooms with one to four bedrooms. The fitness center and on-site spa offer upscale treatment. Three indoor and outdoor pools plus a kiddie complex offer an opportunity to relax. Many guests choose these suites for a business stay as well. Children's programs are supervised for an easy combination of family and business travel. An on-site golf director is well-versed in arranging packages. Holiday specials or monthly stays are offered. The **Cypress Room Restaurant** keeps many guests happy with a big homemade breakfast and fine dinner opportunities. See the "Dining" chapter for details.

LANDMARK RESORT

(1501 S. Ocean Blvd. ☎ 843.448.9441 ⬮ landmarkresort.com)
The choice of rooms and efficiencies in this high-rise ranges
from oceanfront and ocean-view to value-priced standard units.
Its indoor and outdoor pools and putt putt golfing are attractive for family vacations. The expo hall is suitable for trade
shows and the ballroom seats 700. The event and catering staff
welcomes meetings and beach weddings. Holiday, off season
and sporting event specials are offered as are senior and group
discounts and value-priced golf packages.

LONG BAY RESORT

(7200 N. Ocean Blvd. ☎ 843.449.3361 ⬮ longbayresort.com)
Oceanfront condos, suites, rooms, and efficiencies total 286 in
this high-rise oceanfront hotel. The location is a bit north of
the busiest section, and the beach views are expansive. Indoor
and outdoor pools and the lazy river are spacious and offer the
perfect view. Golf and entertainment packages are good value,
and off season or holiday rates quite enticing. Senior and military discounts are offered. **Martin's** restaurant in the hotel is a
long time local favorite and is definitely recommended for daily
breakfast and dinner offered from Monday to Saturday.

MONTEREY BAY SUITES

(6804 N. Ocean Blvd. ☎ 843.449.4833
⬮ montereybaysuites.com) This all-suite hotel is a renovated
boutique hotel on the oceanfront. Indoor, outdoor, and
rooftop pools and decks are spacious; lazy river and kiddie
attractions are also available. The parking deck is attached.
A full daily breakfast is included. Golf packages and winter
rentals up to a 99-day stay are value-priced.

OCEAN REEF RESORT

(7100 N. Ocean Blvd. ☎ 843.449.4441 🖱 oceanreefresort.com)
Additions to this oceanfront property in 2006 included 52
condos of one-, two- and three-bedroom sizes and a kiddies
splash attraction. Additional rooms, suites, and efficiencies
are also available. Seasonal children's activities are supervised
programs. Pools are indoor or outdoor with spacious decks or
lawn chairs for relaxation under the palm trees or gliding along
the covered lazy river. The ballroom or four meeting salons
can accommodate up to 400 persons for weddings or meetings
with planners on staff for assistance. Packages are offered for
golf, last-minute bookings, off season, early booking, holidays,
and entertainment. Senior and military discounts are available.

OCEANS ONE RESORT

(102 S. Ocean Blvd. ☎ 843.626.2033 🖱 oceansoneresort.com)
This resort's south-end location is quieter than other parts of
Myrtle Beach. The one-, two- or three-bedroom oceanfront
condos are spacious, and many of the rooms offer impressive panoramic views. Indoor or outdoor pools, an interactive splash area for kids, a lazy river, and a fitness room
offer enough to keep a vacationing family happy and busy.
Off-season rates offer excellent value.

PATRICIA GRAND

**(2719 N. Ocean Blvd. ☎ 843.448.8453
🖱 patriciagrandonline.com)** This family resort hotel includes
suites, rooms, and efficiencies. The oceanfront pool is large,
and the indoor pool and lazy river are great for year-round
use. A fitness center, business center, and restaurant complete
with a lounge and facing the ocean are useful for adults,

who also find this a convenient drive from the Myrtle Beach Convention Center. Golf and entertainment packages are popular, and special off season rates are quite attractive.

SPRINGMAID BEACH RESORT

(3200 S. Ocean Blvd. ☎ 843.315.7100
📞 springmaidbeach.com) This is a quiet beach location at the south end of Myrtle Beach, between **Springmaid Pier** and the **Myrtle Beach State Park**. See the "Fishing" chapter for information about the pier and the "Attractions" chapter for details. The oceanfront facilities include 500 suites and efficiencies, a private balcony, six pools, and two lazy rivers plus plenty of space on the beach. It's a family-oriented value choice as well as being a business hotel with a conference center. The miniature golf and arcade are assured to keep families entertained. The buffet restaurant is great value, especially for breakfast. Three large ballrooms and an exhibit space are suitable for a variety of weddings or business events, with catering services available. A unique offer of this resort is the watermedia workshop offered each spring and fall. This is an artist's dream, with a full week of instruction and guided painting experiences, with free time spent relaxing on the oceanfront.

YACHTSMAN RESORT HOTEL

(1304 N. Ocean Blvd. ☎ 843.448.2214 📞 yachtsman.com) This timeshare resort offers vacation weeks at resale in all-oceanfront units of one- or two-bedroom efficiencies or suites with full kitchens. An indoor pool and two outdoor pools, plus an activity room are adequate for a family visit. An activities' staff arranges tee times, bingo, ping pong, or shuffleboard tournaments on varying days. In the center of the busy Myrtle Beach area, this is an ideal choice for walking to several restaurants or arcades. **Pier 14** is a busy fishing pier and a recommended restaurant for lunch or dinner with frequent entertainment. Details are in the "Fishing" chapter and the "Dining" chapter.

NORTH STRAND ACCOMMODATIONS

The North Strand listings begin at Barefoot Landing and include the sections north of there, which sometimes are referred to as Windy Hill, Crescent Beach, North Myrtle Beach, Ocean Drive, and Cherry Grove. The city address is North Myrtle Beach for all accommodations mentioned in this section. The North Strand accommodations offer convenient access to North Strand golf courses and dining options.

AVISTA RESORT

(300 N. Ocean Blvd. ☎ 843.249.2521 🖱 avistaresort.com) A 17-floor oceanfront condo tower, Avista Resort offers one- two- or three-bedroom units, full kitchens, a fitness center, indoor and outdoor pools and two lazy rivers. The convenient location, plenty of beach front, a restaurant, and seasonal poolside grill make this a popular choice for families or golfers. Event facilities can accommodate groups of 300 with special packages including wedding planning, tee-time booking or group entertainment at area theaters.

BAY WATCH

(2701 S. Ocean Blvd. ☎ 843.272.4600 🖱 baywatchresort.com) A conference center and family beach resort, this is a convenient location in North Myrtle Beach. Guest accommodations include studio, two-, three- and four-bedroom suites. Nightly, monthly, and weekly winter rentals are offered. Indoor and outdoor pools, an oceanfront lounge, and a restaurant and beach bar are popular with families as well as business guests, who will find convenient meeting, banquet and exhibit space. A business center and fitness center are available. Golf packages offer great deals.

BEACH COVE RESORT

(4800 S. Ocean Blvd. ☎ 800.369.7043 🖱 beachcove.com) It's nice for guests looking for family or business accommodations in North Myrtle Beach. The location is convenient for 320 rooms which are two-room executive suites or two- and three-bedroom condos. The indoor and outdoor pool, as well as the lazy river ride appeals to children. The multi-level oceanfront deck and pool bar appeal to adults. Meeting space to accommodate up to 300 persons was updated in 2009. Seasonal specials are offered.

MAR VISTA GRANDE

(603 S. Ocean Blvd. ☎ 843.663.1246 🖱 marvistagrande.com) These are three- and four-bedroom condos with oceanfront or ocean view choices with complete kitchens and balconies, not to mention good views. Indoor and outdoor pools and lazy river attract family vacationers. Spa, fitness center, game room, and business center are on-site. It's convenient to restaurants and to the popular dance spots for shaggers visiting for special events. Seasonal and holiday specials are suggested.

OCEAN CREEK RESORT

(10600 N Kings. Hwy. ☎ 843.272.7724 🖱 oceancreek.com) Within a gated resort and equipped with full-time security, this is somewhat more private than most other area communities. The tower offers two- or three-bedroom condos which are oceanfront, ocean view, or southern view. Villas, condos, and cottages are popular with family groups, golfers, second-home owners, and a few year-round residents. Summer features are children's activities and golf packages attract fall or spring guests. Pools are oceanfront, indoor or outdoor. The lively oceanfront cabana bar is seasonal. Fitness center, tennis complex, meeting facilities, and restaurant are convenient. A wide variety of off season specials appeal to military, seniors, or one-night guests.

OCEAN DRIVE BEACH & GOLF RESORT
(98 N. Ocean Blvd. ☎ 843.249.1436 🌐 oceandriveresort.com)
This is in the center of the North Myrtle Beach action, including the dance spots for shaggers who convene season- ally and the new oceanfront entertainment pavilion. Units are oceanfront or ocean view. Suites, condos, and efficiencies are also available. Amenities include indoor and outdoor pools, sundecks, sauna, arcade, beauty salon, breakfast café, plus a seasonal tiki bar and grill. The **Spanish Galleon Beach Club** inside this hotel is one of the area's best known nightclubs, which always features a DJ or live entertainment. Expect tradi- tional beach bands such as The Embers, the Craig Woolard Band, the Entertainers, and many similar ones delivering high-energy dance music. The Shaggers Hall of Fame Museum is located here. It's an easy walk to several local eateries for breakfast, lunch, pizza, and ice cream. Plenty of beer, wine, and cocktails are available for thirsty party people. It's a short drive to additional restaurants which are listed in the "Dining" chapter. As many as 300 people can be accommodated for meetings or weddings. A wide variety of pre-packaged golf plans are offered.

PRINCE RESORT

(3500 N. Ocean Blvd. ☎ 843.417.1399 🖱 princeresortonline.com) Adjacent to the popular **Cherry Grove Pier**, this oceanfront resort offers the family atmosphere of Cherry Grove which is a preference for anglers. Spacious condos and plenty of beach access, plus breakfast options at the pier make this an attractive location. The resort has the only two-story observation deck on a privately owned pier, and the view alone is enough to interest photographers as well as water lovers. Golf and off season specials are offered.

SEA SIDE

(2301 S. Ocean Blvd. ☎ 843.272.5166 🖱 seasidemb.com) This oceanfront resort is a boutique condo property offering 69 units of one, two or three bedrooms which are oceanfront or ocean view. Full kitchens and private balconies are in each. Two pools, lazy river and fitness center round out the amenities. It's a couple of miles from the center of activity when the dance crowds converge on North Myrtle Beach, and a shuttle usually runs especially for these events. Golf packages are enticing. Also, ask about sailing charters, a spa escape or a helicopter tour.

SEA WATCH RESORT

(10475 Lake Shore Dr. ☎ 843.918.0000 🖱 seawatchresort.com) Accommodations are all oceanfront with choices of studio, one, two or three bedrooms. All have fully equipped kitchens, and some even have laundry facilities. Amenities are six oceanfront pools including two covered and two heated, two lazy rivers, a game room, an exercise room, and year-round activities for children. Senior and military rates

are offered. Customized or pre-packaged golf trips offer a
variety of courses and rates. Conference space accommodates
weddings or meetings up to 300 guests.

TILGHMAN BEACH & GOLF RESORT

(1819 N. Ocean Blvd. ☎ 843.280.0913 🖱 tilghmanresort.com)
This resort features condo suites with two or three bedrooms
with full kitchens, indoor and outdoor pools, a fitness center,
lazy river, and a water play area for children. It's across the
street from the beach, and some views are of the **Surf Club**
golf course. Special packages are offered for golfers, entertainment, girlfriend getaways, or romantic escapes, as well as family
vacations. Bikers are also welcome. Sailing charters and holiday
packages are available. The snack bar and grill room feature
some of the friendliest staff and tasty fare for breakfast, lunch,
or snacks. Additional restaurants as described in the "Dining"
chapter are convenient.

TOWERS ON THE GROVE

(2100 N. Ocean Blvd. ☎ 843.249.7575 🖱 towersonthegrove.com)
Cherry Grove is the most northern section of the contiguous
beach strand, although Little River, which is on the Intracoastal
Waterway, is the most northern community in South Carolina.
These sections are described in the "Getting To Myrtle Beach"
chapter. This high-rise oceanfront condo resort is central to
Cherry Grove, which has its own loyalists among families and
anglers who choose to return here year after year. The units
are one-, two-, or three-bedroom with private balconies, full
kitchens, and individual laundries. A children's jungle play
area plus lazy river and the partially covered pool are attractive features on the private access walkway onto the beach.

The fitness facility is state-of-the-art. This is convenient to the popular **Cherry Grove Fishing Pier** which is described in the "Fishing" chapter. Golf, girlfriend getaways, spa, and holiday packages are offered. Discounts are available to active or retired military. The non-smoking facility is somewhat unusual in that regard.

WYNDHAM VACATION RESORT

(410 S. Ocean Blvd. ☎ 843.692.9311 🖱 wyndham.com/hotels/ MYROB) One- or two-bedroom suites with full kitchens, private laundry facilities, and private balconies are available in this oceanfront resort. This was previously a Fairfield Inn. A fitness center, game room, playground, and children's activities add to the ambience. There are two indoor pools and three outdoor pools. Daily housekeeping is by request only.

SOUTH STRAND ACCOMMODATIONS

South Strand hotel recommendations are in Garden City, which is south of Myrtle Beach. Tourists to Myrtle Beach who are staying in the southern end can opt for a variety of accommodations in Garden City with a quiet getaway from the crowds in an oceanfront property.

GARDEN CITY INN

(1120 N. Waccamaw Dr., Garden City ☎ 843.651.5600 🖱 gardencityinns.com) This hotel is located to the south of most major attractions and is away from the crowds, and has a family atmosphere. It's ideal for a quiet getaway or for anglers who will be situated between two piers. All guest rooms are oceanfront with private balconies and are furnished with two queen beds. Two penthouse suites feature three bedrooms each. The outdoor pool, large deck, and kiddie pool face the ocean. Plenty of restaurants are nearby in Garden City or Murrells Inlet. See the "Dining" chapter for detailed recommendations.

KINGFISHER INN

(100 N. Waccamaw Dr., Garden City ☎ 843.651.2131 🖱 kingfisher-inn.com) Located away from the center of the busy beach, the Kingfisher Inn is beside one of the fishing piers and ideal for families interested in water sports. Units in this oceanfront hotel are studio, one- or two-bedroom, plus three-bedroom penthouse suites. The outdoor swimming pool is oceanfront, and an exercise room is on-site. Value pricing is attractive for families, golfers, or anglers. It's an easy drive to restaurants throughout the Murrells Inlet area, as well as those nearby in Garden City. Recommended restaurants are described in the "Dining" chapter.

WATERS EDGE RESORT

(1012 N. Waccamaw Dr., Garden City ☎ 843.651.0002 🖱 watersedgeresort.com) The location is near Surfside, but far enough away from the middle of Myrtle Beach to provide quiet time. All units are oceanfront condos of one, two, or three bedrooms with full kitchens. Indoor and outdoor pools, a fitness center, an oceanfront café, and lounge make it suitable for families to stay here. Holiday and shoppers' packages are offered sometimes.

RENTAL COMPANIES

Rental companies are suggested for North Myrtle Beach or Surfside choices of homes, villas, and condos which are often preferred for large family groups or extended stays.

ELLIOTT REALTY

(401 Sea Mountain Hwy., North Myrtle Beach ☎ 843.249.1406 🖰 northmyrtlebeachtravel.com) For rentals of privately owned beach houses, condos, golf villas, or channel-side houses throughout the North Myrtle Beach area, this is one of the large established companies with myriad offers. Winter rentals, special packages, or pet-friendly choices are available. For groups up to 30, large properties are suggested. Linens usually are by special request.

CENTURY 21 THOMAS

(625 Sea Mountain Hwy., North Myrtle Beach ☎ 843.249.2100 🖰 century21thomas.com) Vacation homes and condo rentals in the North Myrtle Beach area are managed by this large company for private property owners. Homes and condos have from one to eight bedrooms and a variety of amenities. All are furnished and equipped, but linens must be ordered if desired. Departure cleaning is provided. Locations are beachfront, channel side, or walking distance to the beach. Monthly and long-term rentals also are handled, and golf packages are offered.

SURFSIDE REALTY

(213 S. Ocean Blvd., Surfside Beach ☎ 843.238.3435
⬤ surfsiderealty.com) To rent homes or condos, particularly on the south end of the strand such as Surfside and Garden City, contact the reputable Surfside Realty, which has 500 rental places on offer. This includes oceanfront, ocean view or second- and third-row properties, which are managed for their owners. Whether for weekly vacations for families or long-term seasonal rentals, the price range and the type of property could suit many tastes.

BED AND BREAKFASTS

Bed and breakfasts are few and far between here. International guests or historic and cultural travelers, who often prefer the quiet or family atmosphere of such accommodations, are not the typical visitors to the Myrtle Beach area. The following are recommended for visitors who may prefer staying a bit away from the beach, for those looking for a romantic hideaway, or for guests planning a stay longer than a typical vacation week. The quiet and comfort could be appreciated by writers or stressed executives needing a true escape.

SERENDIPITY INN

(407 71st Ave., N., Myrtle Beach ☎ 843.449.5268
⬤ serendipityinn.com) This small, mission-style continental inn offers 15 rooms, suites, and apartments with private access and a short walk to the beach. With an outdoor pool and all amenities of a small hotel, the non-smoking inn is comfortable and affordable. Catering is arranged and weddings hosted in the courtyard for groups up to 31 people.

Lodging **193**

THE CYPRESS INN

(16 Elm St., Conway ☎ 843.248.0329 🖱 acypressinn.com) This
is an upscale choice overlooking the Waccamaw River with 12
guest rooms. It's suitable for visitors escaping from the beach
or seeking a romantic site for a small intimate wedding, honey-
moon, anniversary, or other celebration. Amenities are top
notch for the business traveler, and breakfast is hot and homemade. Classes and workshops sometimes are scheduled, and
space for 60 people is offered for group meetings or retreats.

THE MOORE FARM HOUSE

**(3423 S.C. 319, Conway ☎ 843.365.7479
🖱 themoorefarmhouse.com)** The farmhouse built in 1914 offers
four second-floor bedrooms with private whirlpools in two
rooms, and his and her showers in one room with basic facilities in the fourth room. The gourmet breakfast along with
the hospitality and a homey atmosphere of years past create a
warm welcome, and the rural location is ideal for a real escape
from the crowds.

Lodging

More Information

All of the chambers of commerce are interested in welcoming visitors to their respective areas, and information is available via their phone or web site on their individual regions and events which may be located there. Tourism itself respects no borders. Visitors see no lines and can easily travel from one town or area to another within the Myrtle Beach area. However, the chambers can be expected to have complete information only for their territory due to their respective policies of promoting the area under their purview. Therefore, it's advisable to check with more than one chamber of commerce or with the individual attractions or events to confirm details.

MYRTLE BEACH AREA CHAMBER OF COMMERCE AND MYRTLE BEACH AREA CONVENTION AND VISITORS BUREAU

(1200 N. Oak St. ☎ 843.626.7444 ⚫ visitmyrtlebeach.com) The chamber and convention and visitor bureau is a single nonprofit organization. Three official welcome centers serve visitors to the area. Free information is available from more than 1,000 chamber members in the respective welcome centers noted below which this chamber operates.

WELCOME CENTERS

Tourists can get more information about Myrtle Beach by visiting any of the three welcome centers in the area. **The Myrtle Beach Welcome Center** *(1200 N. Oak St. ☎ 843.626.7444 ⚫ visitmyrtlebeach.com)* is open Monday through Friday from 8:30 a.m. until 5:00 p.m. Weekend hours vary with the seasons. Visitors coming by air can access the

Airport Welcome Center *(1100 Jetport Rd.* ☎ *843.626.7444*
visitmyrtlebeach.com), which is open daily from 8:00 a.m. until
7:00 p.m. **The South Strand Welcome Center** *(3401 U.S. 17
Bus. S., Murrells Inlet* ☎ *843.651.1010* *visitmyrtlebeach.com)* is
open from 8:30 a.m. until 5:00 p.m. Monday through Friday.
Hours vary on weekends according to the seasons.

NORTH MYRTLE BEACH CHAMBER OF COMMERCE CONVENTION & VISITOR BUREAU

**(270 U.S. 17 N., North Myrtle Beach ☎ 843.281.2662
northmyrtlebeachchamber.com)** The Welcome Center is open
Monday through Friday from 8:30 a.m. until 5:30 p.m. and on
weekends from 10:00 a.m. until 4:00 p.m. It provides a vast
array of free brochures, maps, and area information from
more than 1,000 members with many of these businesses also
being represented by the **Myrtle Beach Area Chamber of
Commerce**. Souvenir items are offered for sale in the welcome
center and online.

LITTLE RIVER CHAMBER OF COMMERCE

**(1180 U.S. 17 N., Little River ☎ 843.249.6604
littleriverchamber.org)** Information is offered in this small
office from 9:00 a.m. until 5:00 p.m. Monday through Friday.
Details can be obtained from the Internet as well, specifically
for events such as **Oktoberfest**, the **Little River Shrimp
and Jazz Fest**, **Christmas Market,** and any other new
events produced by the chamber in the small river town. See
the "Events" chapter for details on the major annual events.
Many members of this chamber are also members of the
North Myrtle Beach organization.

CONWAY CHAMBER OF COMMERCE

(203 Main St., Conway ☎ 843.248.2273

☋ conwayscchamber.com) More than 750 businesses are represented by this chamber, which showcases their free information in the lobby of their building, conveniently located in the downtown walking district. This chamber is an excellent source of information for events which take place in the downtown and on the riverfront. See the "Events" chapter for details on major annual events within the town.

LORIS CHAMBER OF COMMERCE

(4242 Main St., Loris ☎ 843.756.6030 ☋ lorischambersc.com) This chamber is especially helpful for information about events in the small town of Loris such as the **Loris Bog-Off.**

GEORGETOWN COUNTY CHAMBER OF COMMERCE

(531 Front St., Georgetown ☎ 843.546.8436

☋ visitgeorgetowncountysc.com) Many businesses and activities within the communities of Pawleys Island, Garden City, Litchfield, and Murrells Inlet are actively promoted by this chamber as are the town and county of Georgetown. See the "Events" chapter for details about the **Wooden Boat Show** which is located in the river town of Georgetown.

SOUTH CAROLINA WELCOME CENTER

(2121 U.S. 17, Little River ☎ 843.249.21111

☋ discoversouthcarolina.com) Free information and assistance are offered for travel or reservations anywhere in the state. Days and hours of opening are subject to change seasonally.

More Information

More Information

GOVERNMENT

Any of the government offices has helpful information about the respective laws, official government events or public services, but they rely on their chambers of commerce to provide general tourism information. Visit **City of Myrtle Beach** *(☎ 843.918.1000 🖱 cityofmyrtlebeach.com)*, or **City of North Myrtle Beach** *(1018 Second Ave. S., North Myrtle Beach ☎ 843.280.5555 🖱 n-myrtle-beach.sc.us)* for any details pertaining to the area.

HORRY COUNTY
(1301 Second Ave., Conway ☎ 843.915.5000 🖱 horrycounty.org) The county information is helpful for determining laws which may apply to unincorporated areas such as beaches between the City of Myrtle Beach and the City of North Myrtle Beach. Also, the county is the lead emergency management organization for information in case of hurricane threat, forest fire, or any widespread disaster.

LOCAL MEDIA

Several local newspapers keep visitors updated on what's making news in the region. Most papers are available online as well.

THE SUN NEWS
(914 Frontage Rd., E. ☎ 843.626.8555 🖱 thesunnews.com) The daily newspaper is available free online and for purchase in many locations. It is part of the national newspaper group, the McClatchy Company.

ALTERNATIVES

(721 Seaboard St. ☎ 843.444.5556

🖱 **myrtlebeachalternatives.com and alternatives.sc)** Bi-weekly news magazine, online, and free publication in chambers of commerce, plus racks in hundreds of retail and grocery locations. Eclectic coverage includes upcoming events, particularly music and art throughout a wide three-county area.

NORTH MYRTLE BEACH TIMES

(203 U.S. 17 N., North Myrtle Beach ☎ 843.239.3526

🖱 **nmbtimes.com)** This weekly newspaper published on Thursdays covers local news, primarily of interest to North Myrtle Beach and Loris. It is available free online and for purchase in several North Myrtle Beach locations as well as the North Myrtle Beach Chamber of Commerce.

MYRTLE BEACH HERALD

(4761 U.S. 501 W. ☎ 843.626.3131 🖱 myrtlebeachherald.com) This local newspaper is published weekly on Thursdays and is available free online or for purchase in area grocery and retail shops. It covers general Myrtle Beach area business and local news.

THE HORRY INDEPENDENT

(2510 Main St., Conway ☎ 843.248.6671

🖱 **horryindependent.com)** The weekly newspaper published on Thursdays primarily covers Conway news as well as county news from the courts and county offices which are headquartered in Conway. It is available free online and for purchase in Conway businesses.

GEORGETOWN TIMES

(615 Front St., Georgetown ☎ 843.546.4148 🖱 gtowntimes.com)
This local newspaper is published three times weekly. It is free online and available for purchase in many Georgetown businesses. Coverage of news and events in southern communities such as Pawleys Island is included as well as Georgetown and rural areas. It is free online and for purchase in Georgetown and south strand businesses.

TELEVISION

All network television stations provide news and weather updates accessible via their Internet sites. Television stations in the Myrtle Beach area include ABC Network's WPDE-TV (🖱 *carolinalive.com*), NBC's WMBF-TV (🖱 *wmbfnews.com*), CBS's WBTW-TV (🖱 *scnow.com*), and FOX's WFXB-TV (🖱 *myfoxmyrtlebeach.com*).

About the Authors

The Mitchells have lived in Myrtle Beach since 1992. Their company, The Mitchell Group, Inc., offers marketing consultation to tourism organizations, events, and additional non-profit and professional clients. Charlie and Liz both are freelance writers who have published hundreds of features in regional and national media.

They also own Speakers International, a booking and management agency for professional speakers and entertainers who live and work internationally.

Charlie Mitchell co-authored three annual editions of *Insider's Guide to Golf in the Carolinas*. A native of Lynchburg, Virginia, he also has extensive experience in real estate and teaching in public schools and college.

Liz Mitchell writes several blogs including Flavors of Hilton Head, Brunswick County Vacation Planning and the Beach Bytes series for ◔ *away.com*. She has managed international marketing programs for the Myrtle Beach Area Chamber of Commerce, Myrtle Beach Golf Holiday, and the Beaufort Regional Chamber of Commerce.

They travel, photograph, interview, write, and play anywhere in the world and especially love relaxing in their own beach chairs in Myrtle Beach. Their new work is published regularly at ◔ *TheMitchellGroupInternational.com*.

Index

Index

NOTES:

NOTES:

꙳**tourist town**guides®

Explore America's Fun Places

Books in the *Tourist Town Guides*® series are available at bookstores and online. You can also visit our web site for additional book and travel information. The address is:

http://www.touristtown.com

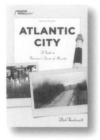

Atlantic City (4th Edition)

This guide will introduce a new facet of Atlantic City that goes beyond the appeal exercised by its lavish casinos. Atlantic City is one of the most popular vacation destinations in the United States.

Price: $14.95; ISBN: 978-1-935455-00-4

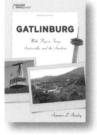

Gatlinburg (2nd Edition)

Whether it is to see the weird and wonderful displays at Ripley's Believe It or Not! Museum, or to get the adrenalin pumping with some outdoor activity or to revel in the extravaganza of Dollywood, people come to the Smokies for a variety of reasons – and they are never disappointed!

Price: $14.95; ISBN: 978-1-935455-04-2

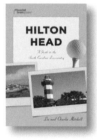

Hilton Head

A barrier island off the coast of South Carolina, Hilton Head is a veritable coastal paradise. This destination guide gives a detailed account of this resort island, tailor made for a coastal vacation.

Price: $14.95; ISBN: 978-1-935455-06-6

Myrtle Beach (2nd Edition)

The sunsets are golden and the pace is relaxed at Myrtle Beach, the beachside playground for vacationers looking for their fill of sun, sand, and surf. Head here for the pristine beaches, the shopping opportunities, the sea of attractions, or simply to kick back and unwind.

Price: $14.95; ISBN: 978-1-935455-01-1

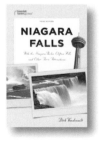

Niagara Falls (3rd Edition)

The spirited descent of the gushing falls may be the lure for you, but in Niagara Falls, it is the smorgasbord of activities and attractions that will keep you coming back for more!

Price: $14.95; ISBN: 978-1-935455-03-5

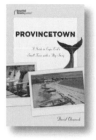

Provincetown

With a rich heritage and proud history, Provincetown is America's oldest art colony, but there is more to this place than its culture. The guide to Provincetown explores its attractions and accommodations, culture and recreation in detail to reveal a vacation destination definitely worth visiting.

Price: $13.95; ISBN: 978-1-935455-07-3

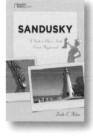

Sandusky

The Cedar Point Amusement Park may be the main reason to visit Sandusky, but this comprehensive guide provides ample reason to stick around and explore Sandusky and the neighboring islands.

Price: $13.95; ISBN: 978-0-9767064-5-8

Williamsburg

The lure to explore history is unmistakable in the town, but Williamsburg is so much more than its rich history. Head to this region to discover the modern facets of this quaint town, indulge in activities guaranteed to hook your interest, and step into the past in this historically significant destination.

Price: $14.95; ISBN: 978-1-935455-05-9

Also Available: (See http://www.touristtown.com for details)

Black Hills	Price: $14.95; ISBN: 978-0-9792043-1-9)
Breckenridge	Price: $14.95; ISBN: 978-0-9767064-9-6)
Frankenmuth	Price: $13.95; ISBN: 978-0-9767064-8-9)
Hershey	Price: $13.95; ISBN: 978-0-9792043-8-8)
Jackson Hole	Price: $13.95; ISBN: 978-0-9792043-3-3)
Key West (2nd Edition)	Price: $14.95; ISBN: 978-1-935455-02-8)
Las Vegas	Price: $13.95; ISBN: 978-0-9792043-5-7)
Mackinac	Price: $14.95; ISBN: 978-0-9767064-7-2)
Ocean City	Price: $13.95; ISBN: 978-0-9767064-6-5)
Wisconsin Dells	Price: $13.95; ISBN: 978-0-9792043-9-5)

www.touristtown.com

ORDER FORM #1
ON REVERSE SIDE

Tourist Town Guides® is published by:
Channel Lake, Inc.
P.O. Box 1771
New York, NY 10156

ORDER FORM

Telephone: With your credit card handy, call toll-free 800.592.1566

Fax: Send this form toll-free to 866.794.5507

E-mail: Send the information on this form to orders@channellake.com

Postal mail: Send this form with payment to Channel Lake, Inc. P.O. Box 1771, New York, NY, 10156

Your Information: ( ) Do not add me to your mailing list

Name: _____

Address: _____

City: _____ State: _____ Zip: _____

Telephone: _____

E-mail: _____

Book Title(s) / ISBN(s) / Quantity / Price
(see previous page or www.touristtown.com for this information)

_____

_____

_____

Total payment*: $_____

Payment Information: (Circle One)   Visa / Mastercard

Number: _____ Exp: _____

Or, make check payable to: **Channel Lake, Inc.**

* Add the lesser of $6.50 USD or 18% of the total purchase price for shipping. International orders call or e-mail first! New York orders add 8% sales tax.

www.touristtown.com

ORDER FORM #2
ON REVERSE SIDE

Tourist Town Guides® is published by:
Channel Lake, Inc.
P.O. Box 1771
New York, NY 10156

ORDER FORM

Telephone: With your credit card handy,
call toll-free 800.592.1566

Fax: Send this form toll-free to 866.794.5507

E-mail: Send the information on this form
to orders@channellake.com

Postal mail: Send this form with payment to Channel Lake, Inc.
P.O. Box 1771, New York, NY, 10156

Your Information: ( ) Do not add me to your mailing list

Name: _____

Address: _____

City: _____ State: _____ Zip: _____

Telephone: _____

E-mail: _____

Book Title(s) / ISBN(s) / Quantity / Price
(see previous page or www.touristtown.com for this information)

_____

_____

_____

Total payment*: $_____

Payment Information: (Circle One) Visa / Mastercard

Number: _____ Exp: _____

Or, make check payable to: **Channel Lake, Inc.**

** Add the lesser of $6.50 USD or 18% of the total purchase price
for shipping. International orders call or e-mail first! New York
orders add 8% sales tax.*